My READ-and-DO Bible Storybook

Debbie Trafton O'Neal

Illustrated by Len Ebert

AUGSBURG • MINNEAPOLIS

To Lindsay, Morgan, and Shannon,
who help me see God's Word
through their eyes

MY READ-AND-DO BIBLE STORYBOOK

Copyright © 1989 Augsburg Fortress

Scripture quotations unless otherwise noted are from the Holy Bible: New International Version. Copyright © 1978 by the New York International Bible Society. Used by permission of Zondervan Bible Publishers.

Line illustrations: RKB Studios

Library of Congress Cataloging-in-Publication Data

O'Neal, Debbie Trafton.
   My read-and-do Bible storybook / Debbie Trafton O'Neal;
illustrated by Len Ebert.
      p.   cm.
   Summary: Presents a collection of Bible stories accompanied by
prayers, songs, fingerplays, handicraft projects, and other
activities.
   ISBN 0-8066-2431-0
   1. Bible stories, English. 2. Activity programs in Christian
education. 3. Children—Prayer-books and devotions—English.
[1. Bible stories. 2. Prayers. 3. Bible crafts.]   I. Ebert, Len,
ill.   II. Title.
BS551.2.054   1989
220.9'505—dc20   89-15184
                                                              CIP
                                                              AC

Manufactured in the U.S.A.   9-2431

93   92   91   90   89   1   2   3   4   5   6   7   8   9   10

Contents

About This Book 5
1   The Beginning of God's World   *Genesis 1:1-25* 7
2   When God Made People   *Genesis 1:26—2:25* 9
3   Noah and the Great Flood   *Genesis 6:9—9:17* 11
4   A Man Named Abraham   *Genesis 12–13, 17–19, 21* 13
5   God's Promise to Abraham   *Genesis 21–22* 17
6   Two Brothers   *Genesis 25, 27–33* 19
7   Joseph and His Rainbow Coat   *Genesis 37, 39–49* 21
8   A Baby Named Moses   *Exodus 2–3* 25
9   God's People in the Wilderness   *Exodus 13–17* 27
10 God's Ten Commandments   *Exodus 19–20* 31
11 The Walls of Jericho   *Joshua 2–5, 5—6:25* 33
12 A Strong Man Named Samson   *Judges 13–16* 37
13 Ruth and Naomi   *Ruth 1–4* 39
14 A Boy Named Samuel   *1 Samuel 1–4, 7–8* 43
15 Saul, the King   *1 Samuel 9–11, 13–15* 45
16 David, the Shepherd Boy and King   *1 Samuel 16–17* 47
17 The Book of Psalms   *Selected psalms* 49
18 The Book of Proverbs   *Selected proverbs* 53
19 Solomon, the Wise King   *1 Kings 3, 5–10* 55
20 Elijah, One of God's Prophets   *1 Kings 17:1-16* 57
21 Daniel and the Lions   *Daniel 6* 61
22 Jonah and the Big Fish   *Jonah 1–4* 63
23 Isaiah Tells about God   *Isaiah 9:1-7; 11:1-9* 67
24 The Birth of John   *Luke 1:5-25, 57-80* 69
25 Mary, the Mother of Jesus   *Luke 1:26-56* 71
26 Jesus Is Born!   *Luke 2:1-7* 73
27 The Shepherds Visit Jesus   *Luke 2:8-20* 75
28 The Wise Men Who Followed a Star   *Matthew 2:1-12* 77
29 Jesus Visits the Temple   *Luke 2:41-52* 79
30 A Man Named John   *Matthew 3:1-17* 83
31 The Four Fishermen   *Luke 5:1-11* 85
32 Twelve Special Friends   *Matthew 10:1-42; Luke 6:12-16* 89
33 Jesus Teaches the People   *Matthew 5:1-12; Luke 6:17-26* 91
34 A Boat in a Storm   *Mark 4:35-41* 93

35   Five Loaves of Bread and Two Fish   *John 6:1-15* 95

36   Jesus and the Children   *Mark 10:13-16* 97

37   The Good Neighbor   *Luke 10:25-37* 99

38   Zacchaeus, a Tax Collector   *Luke 19:1-10* 101

39   The Lost Sheep   *Luke 15:1-7* 103

40   The Lost Coin   *Luke 15:8-10* 107

41   The Lost Son   *Luke 15:11-32* 109

42   A Woman Who Loved God   *Luke 21:1-4* 111

43   A Special Prayer   *Luke 11:1-13* 113

44   The Good Shepherd   *John 10:1-18* 115

45   A Parade to Welcome Jesus   *Matthew 21:1-11* 117

46   A Night When Jesus Was a Servant   *Luke 22:7-23; John 13:1-17* 119

47   Jesus' Trial and Death   *Mark 15:1-47; Luke 22:47—23:56* 121

48   Jesus Is Alive!   *Mark 16:1-8; Luke 24:1-12* 123

49   A Rushing Wind   *Acts 2:1-41* 125

50   The Church Long Ago   *Acts 2:42-47* 127

About This Book

This Bible storybook is for families to read together. Written in an easy-to-read style at the interest level of young children, it offers families an opportunity to share God's Word in meaningful ways with one another.

Children learn best experientially, especially through sensory and active learning experiences. Unique features of this Bible story book are the family activities and prayers that follow each Bible story. These activities include songs to sing, fingerplays to share, and other activities to do together. Each time a Bible story is followed by an activity that relates to it directly, children will better remember the story and it will become a meaningful part of their lives.

Families in today's world are busy people. My prayer for your family is that through God's Word and the time you spend sharing this book together, your love for God and for one another will grow to its full potential.

Debbie Trafton O'Neal

1 The Beginning of God's World

Genesis 1:1-25

This Bible story is about the beginning of God's world.

In the beginning there was nothing but empty darkness. But God was there.

God said, "Let there be light." And God made a great light to shine in the darkness. God made the daytime and the nighttime. "This is good," God said. And it was the first day in God's world.

On the second day God made the land and sky. "This is good," God said.

On the third day God made the sea and the dry land. God made many trees and plants to grow on the land. God made evergreen trees and apple trees. God made red, yellow, and purple flowers. "This is good," God said.

On the fourth day God said, "Let lights shine in the sky for daytime and nighttime." God made the warm, golden sun to shine in the daytime. God made the cool, silver moon to light up the sky at night. God made the stars to twinkle and shine with the moon in the nighttime. "This is good," God said.

Then God made living creatures of all kinds to live in the water and in the air. Dolphins and whales and fish swam in the sea. Robins and hummingbirds and parrots flew in the sky. God saw all the living things and said, "This is good." And it was the fifth day in God's world.

On the sixth day God made more living creatures. God made animals to walk on the land—cows and giraffes and turtles. And God said, "This is good."

From the empty darkness God made the world. God's world was filled with warm light and many colors. God's world was filled with the happy sounds of life. And God loved the world. But God was not done making things. That is what our next story is about.

Block walk

Take a walk through your neighborhood with your child. As you walk, point out signs of God's loving creation—a blooming plant, white clouds racing across the blue sky, a raindrop on a shiny green leaf. Notice how many things you see that remind you of God's love.

Prayer to share

Dear God, thank you for filling the world with colors and sounds. Thank you for making it a warm and happy place to live. Amen.

"God saw all that he had made, and it was very good."   *Genesis 1:31*

2   When God Made People

Genesis 1:26—2:25

This Bible story is about when God made people.

God saw the world and said, "This is good."

God saw the warm, golden sun shining in the daytime. God saw the cool, silver moon and the twinkling stars at night.

God saw the living things filling the land and sky and sea with color and sound and life. But God was not finished yet.

God decided to make a man.

First God took dust from the land. God molded the man from the dust. Then God breathed into the man and the man stood up. "I will name you Adam," God said.

God took Adam into a beautiful garden. God said to Adam, "This garden is called Eden. I have made this garden for you. This garden has good soil to grow things in. It has four clear, cool rivers to drink from. This garden has food for you to eat and trees for you to rest under."

Then God brought the animals and birds to Adam.

Adam watched the animals and birds play. Adam gave names to all the animals—the monkeys, the rabbits, and the kangaroos. Adam gave names to all the birds—the toucans, the sparrows, and the flamingos. Adam played with the animals and birds. But Adam was lonely.

So God made a woman to live in the garden with Adam. Adam named the woman Eve. Adam and Eve loved each other. Adam and Eve loved God. Together they played with the animals and birds and took care of God's world. And it was the sixth day in God's world.

After God made people to live in the world, God rested. And it was the seventh day in God's world.

Myself

Lay out a large sheet of butcher paper or newsprint on the floor. Have your child lie down on the paper. Trace your child's outline onto the paper with a crayon or felt-tipped marker. Then help your child draw his or her facial features, hair, and clothing on the body shape. As you are working together, talk about the wonderful bodies God has given us. Hang your child's completed body picture on your refrigerator or a door in your home.

Prayer to share

Dear God, thank you for giving us bodies that can run, jump, sing, eat, sleep, and play in your world. Amen.

"Whenever the rainbow appears in the clouds, I will see it and remember."

Genesis 9:16

3 Noah and the Great Flood

Genesis 6:9—9:17

This Bible story is about Noah and the great flood.

Noah was a man who loved God. Noah and his family were happy in the world God had created. But other people in God's world were not like Noah and his family. They did not love God.

One day God said to Noah, "I am not happy with the way people are hurting each other in my world. I am going to cover the earth with a great flood."

Then God said to Noah, "I want you and your family to build an ark. Build the ark from strong wood. Put a big door in the side of the ark."

Then God said to Noah, "Take your family into the ark. And take two of every bird, two of every animal, and two of every creature that crawls on the earth into the ark with you. Bring enough food for everyone to share. I promise to take care of you."

Noah did what God had said. When the ark was finished, Noah and his family took two of each bird and animal and two of each crawling creature from God's world into the ark.

The pigeons flew into the ark—*whirrr.* The boas slithered into the ark—*ssssss.* The cows chewed their cud as they plodded into the ark—*clomp, clomp, clomp.*

When everything was ready, God shut the door. And the rain began to fall.

Plop. Plop. Plop.
Pitter-patter-pitter-patter.

Rat-tat-a-tat-tat.
Rat-tat-a-tat-tat.

It rained in God's world for 40 days and 40 nights. But Noah's family and all the living creatures—two of every kind—were safe and dry inside the ark.

Water covered the earth for 150 days. God remembered Noah and his family. God remembered the birds. God remembered the animals. God remembered all the other living creatures.

Then God sent a wind over the earth to dry up the water. Finally Noah sent a dove out of the ark. But the dove could not find dry land, and it came back to Noah. Noah waited seven days and then he sent out the dove again. When the dove came back to Noah, there was an olive leaf in its beak. It had found a tree top. Seven days later Noah sent out the dove again. This time it did not come back. It had found dry land.

Then God said to Noah, "Open the door. Bring your family and every living creature with you out into my world."

When Noah and every living creature came out of the ark, Noah and his family gave thanks to God. God was pleased.

God said to Noah, "This is my promise. Never again will a flood cover the earth. My rainbow in the clouds will remind us of this."

Noah thought about what God had said. And Noah was happy to live in God's world.

"Who Built the Ark?"

Sing this song with your child:

Refrain F / C7 / F

Who built the ark? No-ah! No-ah! Who built the ark? Broth-er

C7 / Fine F / C

No-ah built the ark. 1. Old man No-ah built the ark, he

G7 / C

built it out of the hick-o-ry bark. He built it long, both

to Refrain G7 / C

wide and tall with plen-ty of room for the large and small.

2 In came the animals, two by two,
   hippopotamus and kangaroo.
   In came the animals, three by three,
   two big cats and a bumblebee. *Refrain.*

3 In came the animals, four by four,
   two through the window and two through the
     door.
   In came the animals, five by five,
   The bees came swarming from the hive.
   Refrain.

4 In came the animals, six by six,
   elephant laughed at the monkey's tricks.

   In came the animals, seven by seven,
   Giraffes and camels lookin' up to heaven.
   Refrain.

5 In came the animals, eight by eight,
   some on time and the others late.
   In came the animals, nine by nine,
   Some were laughin' and some were cryin'.
   Refrain.

6 In came the animals, ten by ten,
   time for the voyage to begin.
   Noah said, "Go shut the door,
   the rain's started fallin' and we can't take more."
   Refrain.

Words: Based on Genesis 6, 7   Music: Spiritual

Prayer to share

Make a rainbow prayer with your child. From colored paper cut simple shapes such as a red apple, yellow sun, or a blue bird. Write a prayer of thanks on a large sheet of paper, inserting the shapes you have made in place of names of things for which you are thankful. Use this prayer as a special family prayer.

4   A Man Named Abraham

Genesis 12–13, 17–19, 21

This Bible story is about a man named Abraham.

A long time ago, Abraham and his wife Sarah lived in the land of Haran. Abraham and Sarah loved and trusted God.

Abraham and Sarah had many animals—sheep and goats and cows. There were many people who helped Abraham and Sarah take care of their sheep and goats and cows. These people loved and trusted God too.

One day God said to Abraham, "Leave your home and go to a land I will show you. Take your sheep and goats and cows with you. Take the people who help you care for your animals too. I will bless you and make your name great. All people will remember you and bless you."

Because Abraham and Sarah loved and trusted God, they obeyed. They traveled a long way to the land God showed them. When they got to the new land, Abraham and Sarah and all the people, too, thanked God for being with them.

But Abraham and Sarah wondered about the things God had told them. How would all people remember them? They did not even have children who would remember them! God told Abraham, "You and Sarah will have a child." Abraham laughed because they were getting too old to have children.

One day a long time later, Abraham was sitting outside his tent. When he looked up, Abraham saw three men standing in front of him.

Abraham brought water for the hot, tired men.

He asked Sarah to make bread for the men to eat. And Abraham shared other food with them.

After the men had eaten, they told Abraham, "God has sent us to give you a message. You and Sarah will have a baby."

This time Sarah laughed, because she and Abraham were old enough to be grandparents. But just as God had said, they had a baby.

Abraham said to Sarah, "Our son's name will be Isaac."

"Yes," said Sarah. "Isaac means 'laughter.' Isaac, our son, will bring happiness and laughter to our lives."

Then Abraham and Sarah thanked God for always keeping promises.

In our tent

Use a blanket to make a tent. Drape the blanket over a table, either in your home or outside. Let your child help you prepare a simple snack, such as raisins and wheat crackers or bread and cheese. Share the snack together in your tent, in much the same way that Abraham would have shared a snack with the three visitors. Talk about

14

promises that we make to each other, the promises that God made to Abraham, and the promises that God makes to us.

Prayer to share

Dear God, we thank you for always taking care of us as you took care of Abraham and Sarah. We love and trust you too. Amen.

5 God's Promise to Abraham

Genesis 21–22

This Bible story is about God's promise to Abraham.

When God told Abraham and Sarah they would have a son, they were happy! When their son was born, they named him Isaac. God had kept the promise!

Abraham and Sarah loved Isaac. Isaac grew up loving his parents and loving God.

One day, God called to Abraham. Abraham heard God and answered, "Here I am."

Then God said, "Abraham, take your son, Isaac, whom you love, to the mountains. I want to know how much you love me. I want you to offer your son Isaac as a sacrifice."

God's words troubled Abraham. But Abraham loved and trusted God. Very early the next morning, Abraham woke up and saddled a donkey. Then he woke up Isaac and two servants to go with him.

When they reached a place with many trees, Abraham and the servants cut wood for the sacrifice. Isaac tied the wood on the donkey's back.

After walking for three days, Abraham and Isaac saw the mountains. Then Abraham said to the servants, "Stay here with the donkey. Isaac and I will go farther up the mountain to worship God."

Abraham took the wood from the donkey's back and gave it to Isaac to carry. Abraham carried the fire for the sacrifice. As they walked up the mountain, Isaac asked, "We have the fire and the wood, Father, but where is the lamb for sacrifice?"

And Abraham, who loved and trusted God, answered, "God will provide the lamb, my son."

When they reached the place God had told Abraham about, Abraham built an altar. Isaac put the wood on top. Then Abraham, who loved and trusted God, laid his son Isaac on top of the altar.

But God called out, "Abraham! Abraham! Do not harm Isaac. Now I know how much you love and trust me. You would even give me your son. Look over there."

When Abraham looked up, he saw a ram caught in the bushes. Abraham helped Isaac down and together they put the ram on the altar. Then Abraham and Isaac worshiped God.

God loves us

God loved Abraham and Isaac very much. God loves us too. Cut a heart shape from a clean, damp sponge. Clip a clothespin in the center. Have your child dip the heart into tempera paint and "print" hearts on a sheet of paper in a random pattern. When the paint dries, print "God loves us" on the paper. Hang the heart prints where you will see it often.

Prayer to share

Dear God, thank you for loving us. Help us to share your love with our friends. Amen.

"But Esau ran to meet Jacob and embraced him."　　　*Genesis 33:4*

6　Two Brothers

Genesis 25, 27–33

This Bible story is about two brothers. Isaac grew up and married Rebekah. They were very happy because they loved God and knew that God loved them. There was only one thing that made Isaac and Rebekah sad—they did not have any children.

Then God answered their prayers! Isaac and Rebekah had twin sons, Esau and Jacob.

Esau was the son born first. Esau had rough skin and red hair. Esau liked to be outside where he could hunt with his sling and his bow and arrows.

Jacob was born right after Esau. Jacob didn't look like Esau. And Jacob didn't like to hunt.

When Isaac was very old, he called to Esau. "My son, I am getting old. Take your arrows and hunt. Then cook me the tasty food I like best. After that, I can give you my blessing."

Esau hurried to find his bow and arrows. But Rebekah had heard Isaac talking to Esau. She wanted her favorite son, Jacob, to have Isaac's blessing. Rebekah knew that the son who received Isaac's blessing would become the head of the family and would be given most of Isaac's things.

Rebekah thought of a way to trick Isaac and Esau.

First Rebekah cooked the tasty food that Isaac liked. Next she helped Jacob tie rough goatskins on his smooth hands and arms. Then Rebekah borrowed some of Esau's clothes for Jacob to wear.

Jacob went into Isaac's tent. Isaac was very old and almost blind. He could not see Jacob. So Jacob told his father he was Esau. Jacob let his father touch the goatskins on his arms. Isaac thought it was Esau's rough skin. Jacob fed his father the tasty food.

Then Isaac blessed Jacob with these words: "May God bless you and may people respect you. Someday you will be the head of a large family. Let everyone who blesses you be blessed also."

Later, Esau returned home from hunting. When he discovered what Jacob had done, Esau was very angry!

Jacob ran away to another country. There Jacob got married and had many children. Jacob became very rich.

Many years later, Jacob thought about how much God loved him and had taken care of him. Jacob was sorry that he had tricked his father and his brother, Esau.

Jacob looked at his flocks of sheep and his herds of cattle. He chose the best animals he had. Then he went back home to see his brother, Esau.

When Jacob saw Esau, he bowed low to the ground. But Esau ran to Jacob and hugged him.

"I'm sorry I tricked our father and you," Jacob told Esau. "I want to give you my best animals to show you how sorry I am."

But Esau told Jacob, "I am so happy to see you again! You are my brother and I forgive you."

A tasty dish to cook

Work together with your child to prepare this recipe for a family meal. As you work, talk about the tasty dish that Isaac wanted. And talk about the story of two brothers and forgiveness.

This dish can cook all day in a crockpot or slow cooker or in a 350° oven for several hours.

Ingredients:
6 to 8 average size potatoes, peeled and thinly sliced
1 large onion, chopped
2 to 3 carrots, peeled and sliced
1 lb. ground meat, browned
1 15-oz. can of stewed tomatoes and juice
Seasoning to taste

Help your child to layer half of the potatoes, half of the ground meat, half of the onion, half of the carrots, and half of the tomatoes in the pot. Season with salt, pepper, or your favorite spices such as garlic, oregano, or thyme. Repeat the layers of ingredients. Cook on HIGH until the ingredients are heated through, then turn the temperature setting to MEDIUM. The dish is done when the vegetables are tender.

Prayer to share

Before you eat this meal together, pray this prayer:

Thank you, God, for this food we share. Thank you, God, for your loving care. Amen.

"Give thanks to the Lord, for he is good."   *Psalm 136:1*

7 Joseph and His Rainbow Coat

Genesis 37, 39–49

This Bible story is about Joseph and his rainbow coat.

Jacob lived in a land called Canaan. He had 12 sons. Of all his sons, Jacob loved Joseph best. Jacob gave Joseph a beautiful coat of rainbow colors. When Joseph's brothers saw the coat with all the colors of the rainbow, they were jealous.

One day, Jacob sent Joseph out to the fields where his brothers were watching the sheep.

"Look, here comes Joseph," said the brothers. "Let's take his coat of rainbow colors. Then let's throw him in this empty well."

One of the brothers planned to rescue Joseph later. But instead of helping Joseph out of the well, the brothers sold him to men going to Egypt. Then they told their father that Joseph had been killed by a wild animal. Jacob was very sad.

Joseph worked hard in Egypt. But Joseph was put into prison—for something he didn't do.

While Joseph was in prison, he was not afraid. Joseph knew that God loved him and would take care of him.

God helped Joseph to understand many things while he was in prison. In the time when Joseph lived, God sometimes spoke through people's dreams. With God's help, Joseph told people what their dreams meant.

One day, Pharaoh, the ruler of Egypt, said to Joseph, "I had a dream that I do not understand. Can you tell me what it means?"

"I cannot," Joseph answered, "but God can."

In Pharaoh's dream, God showed Joseph there would be seven years of plenty, with more food than people could eat. Then there would be seven years of famine. During the famine, people would be hungry because not enough food would grow.

Because Joseph helped Pharaoh understand his dream, Pharaoh asked Joseph to be the governor of Egypt. Pharaoh knew that God would help Joseph take care of Egypt.

During the seven years of plenty, Joseph collected the extra food the people did not eat. When the famine came, people in Egypt were not hungry because they ate the food Joseph had saved.

But there was not enough food in Canaan where Joseph's family lived. So Joseph's brothers came to Egypt to buy food.

Joseph knew who his brothers were, but they did not know him. Joseph sold food to them and they went back to their home. But soon the food was gone.

The brothers came back to Egypt again. This time Joseph told his brothers who he was. They were afraid Joseph might hurt them because of what they had done to him long before. But Joseph said, "Don't be afraid! I am not angry. God has always taken care of me. God sent me to Egypt to help people during this famine."

Then Joseph said to his brothers, "Go home to Canaan. Bring our family to Egypt. God will take care of us here."

21

A rainbow coat

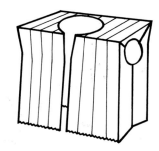

Use a large, brown paper bag to help your child make a rainbow coat like Joseph's. Cut the bag as shown in the diagram to fit your child like an open coat or vest. Have your child decorate the coat with crayons or felt-tipped markers in a combination of stripes or other designs. As you are working together, talk about the story of Joseph.

Prayer to share

Dear God, thank you for loving us and forgiving us when we do wrong things. Like Joseph, help us to love and forgive each other. Amen.

8   A Baby Named Moses

Exodus 2–3

This Bible story is about a baby named Moses.

A long time after Joseph and his brothers died, there was a new Pharaoh in Egypt. This Pharaoh did not know about Joseph. He was afraid of all the descendants of Joseph's family because he thought they would fight against him. So Pharaoh made God's people slaves. Then he decided that none of their baby boys should live.

Moses' mother was one of God's people. She wanted her baby boy to live. She decided to hide baby Moses so Pharaoh would not find him. First she wove a basket with papyrus reeds. Then she put tar and pitch all over the basket so it would float on water. Then Moses' mother put a soft cloth inside the basket for him to sleep on. She put baby Moses in the basket and put the basket in some reeds at the edge of the Nile River.

Then baby Moses' mother gave Miriam, his sister, a special job. Miriam was to watch after baby Moses as he floated in the river.

One day, Pharaoh's daughter came to the river. She saw the basket with baby Moses in it. He was crying.

"This baby is one of God's people," Pharaoh's daughter said. She lifted the basket out of the water. Moses stopped crying.

Then Miriam ran from her hiding place. She bowed before Pharaoh's daughter and asked, "Shall I go and get a woman to care for this baby?"

"Yes, go," answered Pharaoh's daughter.

So Miriam ran to get her mother.

When Miriam and her mother came, Pharaoh's daughter did not know that the woman was baby Moses' mother.

"Will you care for this baby for me?" she asked Miriam's mother. "Love him and take good care of him and I will pay you."

So Moses' mother took good care of Moses until he grew bigger. Then Moses went to the palace to live with Pharaoh's daughter.

When Moses grew up, he saw that the people from Egypt treated God's people unfairly. Once he saw an Egyptian man beating one of God's people. This made Moses very angry. He killed the Egyptian man. Then Moses was afraid. He went far away to live.

One day Moses came to a great mountain of God. Suddenly, a bush burst into flames!

The bush is on fire but it is not burning up! Moses thought. *I will go closer to see it.*

Then a voice called from the bush, "Moses! Moses!"

"Here I am," Moses answered, looking around.

"Do not come closer," the voice said. "Take off your sandals. This is holy ground. I am the God of your father." Then God told Moses, "I will help you lead my people out of Egypt."

God told Moses about a good land where the people would be happy. Because Moses loved and trusted God, he obeyed.

A woven belt

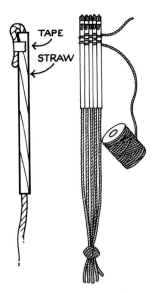

Help your child to weave a simple belt in much the same way Moses' mother may have woven the basket she put him in. Use four or five plastic drinking straws for each belt. Cut five pieces of string or yarn twice the size you want the belt to be. Thread each string through a straw, then tape the end. Tie all the strings at the bottom to make a tassel.

Hold the straws in your left hand. Tie a different colored string to the first straw. Work the string back and forth, over and under the straws. As the weaving fills the straws, push it down onto the strings about an inch at a time. When you reach the end, cut off the straws and tie a tassel at the other end.

Prayer to share

Dear God, we thank you for people who love and take care of us. We thank you for people who show us they care in special ways. Amen.

9 God's People in the Wilderness

Exodus 13–17

This Bible story is about God's people in the wilderness.

God chose Moses to lead God's people, the Israelites, out of Egypt. When Pharaoh said the people could go, they had many things to get ready. God's people did not know how long they would be traveling.

Quickly, quickly—God's people took down their tents.

Quickly, quickly—God's people gathered their flocks of sheep and herds of goats.

Quickly, quickly—God's people packed food to eat.

But God's people did not have time to let their bread rise before they baked it. When they baked the bread, it was flat. After that, every time God's people ate the flat bread, they remembered how quickly they left Egypt.

Moses trusted God to help him lead the people. God led Moses and the people around the desert by the Red Sea.

After a while, Pharaoh changed his mind about letting God's people go. He thought, "If the Israelites are gone, who will do all the work in Egypt?"

So Pharaoh and his army chased God's people through the desert. But God was with them. God said to Moses, "Stretch your hand out over the sea. When the waters move apart, lead my people through."

When Pharaoh's army saw God's people walking through the sea on dry land, they tried to follow. But Moses stretched his hand out over the water again and it covered Pharaoh's army.

For a while the people rejoiced that God had protected them. Then they began to grumble and complain: "We are tired of living in the desert! We are hungry! We should have stayed in Egypt. We had all the food we could eat there."

God heard the people in the wilderness. God told Moses, "I have heard the people grumbling. I know they are tired and hungry. This is what I will do for my people—I will give them bread from heaven."

God told Moses what the people should do with this special bread. Moses told God's people, "God has heard your grumbling. Listen to what God will do because God loves you! God will send bread from heaven—it will come from the sky like rain. Every day, gather enough bread to eat. On the sixth day, gather enough bread for two days, so that you can worship God on the Sabbath. But do not gather any extra bread on any other day."

Some of God's people disobeyed and gathered extra bread. The next morning, it was rotten. Moses reminded the people, "God will take care of us every day—if we love and obey."

God's people, the Israelites, traveled through the wilderness for 40 years. And every day they ate manna, the sweet bread God gave them.

Make your own flatbread

With your child, mix up this simple, slightly sweet flatbread recipe to share.
Cream together ½ cup sugar, ½ cup butter, and 1 teaspoon salt.
Add 1 teaspoon of baking soda to 1½ cups of buttermilk.
Combine creamed mixture and buttermilk with 2 cups oatmeal and 3 cups flour.
Mix thoroughly. Divide the dough into two parts, then roll it out onto a floured surface until it is thin. Bake on an ungreased baking sheet at 350° for 5-8 minutes or until lightly browned. Cool; break into smaller pieces. It tastes good spread with butter and honey!

Prayer to share

Thank you, God, for good bread to eat! Thank you, God, for the people who make our bread. Amen.

10   God's Ten Commandments

Exodus 19–20

This Bible story is about God's Ten Commandments.

God's people were tired of traveling. The grandmothers and grandfathers were tired. The mothers and fathers were tired. All of the children were tired. Even the flocks of sheep and herds of goats were tired of traveling.

"Here is Mount Sinai," Moses told the tired people. "Put up your tents in front of the mountain. Build your fires and bake your bread. Then you can rest."

Moses was tired, too. But Moses wanted to talk with God. While the tired people were busy, Moses went up on the mountain. God told Moses to tell the Israelites that if they would obey God, of all the nations in the world they would be God's treasured people. They would be a holy nation.

When Moses went back down the mountain, the people were resting. Moses called the people together and told them all that God had said. The people told Moses, "We will do everything that God has told you."

Moses went back up the mountain to tell God what the people said. God told Moses, "I am going to talk to you in a thick cloud. Then my people will hear me speaking and they will always put their trust in you."

The day came for Moses and the people to hear what God had to say.

"*Baa, baa*," the sheep cried. They were frightened.

"*Bleat, bleat*," cried the goats. They were frightened too. Even though it was morning, the sky was dark and stormy. Thunder rumbled and lightning flashed in the sky. And God's people saw a thick, dark cloud by the mountain.

God's people waited at the bottom of the mountain while Moses climbed to the top. Moses stopped where the thick cloud was.

God spoke these words to Moses:

I am the Lord your God who brought you out of Egypt.

You shall not have any gods before me.

You shall not make or worship idols.

You shall not use my name in any way that is wrong.

Remember to rest and worship God on the Sabbath day. It is a holy day.

Love and respect your mother and father.

You shall not kill.

You shall not commit adultery.

You shall not steal.

You shall not tell lies about people.

You shall not wish to have things that belong to someone else.

When God spoke, people heard more thunder and saw more lightning. They were afraid!

But Moses said to the people, "Do not be afraid. God loves you! These commandments will help you live the life that God wants you to live."

31

Family rules

Talk with your child about the Ten Commandments or rules that God gave to the Israelites. Emphasize that these rules were intended to help God's people live a safe and happy life together. Continue talking about rules and the need for them in your family and in your community. You might want to make a simple chart of God's rules to post in your home. Use simple words or pictures to represent each rule.

Prayer to share

Dear God, thank you for loving us. Help us to follow your good rules so that we can live a safe and happy life. Amen.

11   The Walls of Jericho

Joshua 2–3, 5—6:25

This Bible story is about what God did to the walls of Jericho.

After Moses died, God chose Joshua to lead the Israelites. God told Joshua that Jericho and the land around it was where God's people should live. The city of Jericho was surrounded on every side by large walls of stone. Joshua thought about how his people could knock down the walls and take this city.

"I will send two men into the city of Jericho," Joshua thought. "They can tell me what the city is like."

Two men went inside the city. When the soldiers of Jericho started looking for the men, a woman named Rahab hid them on her roof.

"Thank you for helping us," the two men said to Rahab. "When we take this city, we will save you and your family."

Late that night, the two men sneaked out of the city. Quickly they ran to find Joshua. Then God told Joshua what to do.

Joshua and the people moved their tents outside the city of Jericho. Then, they waited.

One morning, Joshua's soldiers started marching around the city walls. Seven priests blew trumpets of ram's horns and marched. Two priests carried a box called an ark. Inside the ark were stone tablets with God's commandments on them. After they had marched around Jericho, the soldiers and priests went back to their tents.

This happened the next day and the next day—for six days. "What are the Israelites doing?" wondered the people inside the walls of Jericho. "What does this mean?"

On the seventh day, the soldiers marched. The priests blew their trumpets. Two priests carried the ark. And the people inside the walls of Jericho watched. They thought that the Israelites would stop marching and go back to their tents.

But this time, they didn't stop marching! This time God's people marched around the walls of Jericho once. Then they marched around the walls of Jericho again and again. They marched around the city seven times. Then they stopped. Everything was quiet.

Suddenly, the priests blew the trumpets. All of God's people shouted as loudly as they could.

The walls began to shake. *Rumble, rumble, rumble.* Then with a CRASH the walls of Jericho started tumbling down. Stones and dust were everywhere. The walls of Jericho were destroyed.

Joshua's soldiers rushed into the dust. They found Rahab and her family. God's people took Rahab and her family to their tents. God's people had kept their promise. So had God.

The walls came tumbling down

Reenact the story by building walls with homemade blocks. Make blocks by stuffing large grocery bags with crumpled newspaper. Tape or staple the ends shut.

Construct the wall and march around seven times. Then shout and knock down the walls. Talk about the story.

Prayer to share

Dear God, thank you for always guiding us and protecting us. Thank you, too, for always keeping your promises. Amen.

12   A Strong Man Named Samson

Judges 13–16

This Bible story is about a strong man named Samson.

God sent an angel to tell a woman and her husband they would have a son. "Do not cut your son's hair," the angel said. "His long hair will be a sign that your son is a special person whom God loves."

The woman and her husband waited and waited. When their son was born, the woman said, "Our son is a special person whom God loves. His name will be Samson."

As Samson grew, his mother and father told him that God loved him very much. They never cut Samson's hair. Samson's mother and father knew that his hair was a sign of God's special love.

When Samson grew up he did the things that other men did. But Samson was different from other men. God gave Samson great strength to do many things.

One day Samson was traveling to another city. *"Rooaarr!"* When Samson looked up, he saw a young lion on the road in front of him! With only his hands, Samson killed the lion.

Another time, a thousand Philistine soldiers tried to capture Samson. But God gave Samson strength. With a bone, Samson struck down all the soldiers.

Some time later, Samson met a beautiful woman named Delilah. She was a Philistine. Samson loved Delilah very much. Now the leaders of the Philistines were afraid of Samson and his great strength. They had heard about the lion that Samson had killed with only his hands. They had heard about the other things Samson had done too.

"Listen to us," the Philistines said to Delilah. "Find out why Samson is so strong. We will give you silver. Then you will be very rich."

So Delilah thought about how she could trick Samson. When Delilah asked Samson, "Why are you so strong?" Samson did not tell her the truth.

"If anyone ties me with seven strings, I will be as weak as other men," Samson told Delilah. When Samson was asleep, Delilah tied him with seven strings. But when the Philistines came to take Samson away, he broke the strings.

Samson tricked Delilah and the Philistines several more times. Finally Samson told Delilah the truth.

"The hair on my head has never been cut," Samson said. "If it is cut off, I will be as weak as any other man."

The next time Samson fell asleep, Delilah had someone cut off Samson's hair. Now Samson was weak. The Philistines captured him and put him into prison. But the hair on his head began to grow right away.

The leaders of the Philistines gathered everyone in the city together to celebrate. Samson stood near the pillars of the temple. Samson prayed, "Please, God, make me strong one more time!"

Then Samson reached for the pillars. CRASH! The walls of the temple collapsed. God had made Samson strong one more time.

Samson puppet

Make a puppet of Samson from a paper lunch bag. Help your child draw Samson's face and clothing on the bag with crayons or felt-tipped markers. Glue or staple paper strips or thick yarn to the bag for Samson's hair. You may want to make another puppet character, perhaps one of Samson's parents or Delilah, to use as you retell the story.

Prayer to share

Dear God, thank you for making us special in our own way! Help us to share your love through the words we say and the things we do every day. Amen.

13   Ruth and Naomi

Ruth 1–4

This Bible story is about Ruth and Naomi.

Long ago there was a famine in the land where God's people lived. Because there was no food for the people to eat, many moved to different cities and even to different countries.

A man named Elimelech and his wife Naomi took their two sons with them to the country of Moab. After a time, Elimelech died. Then only Naomi and her two sons were left. Soon, the two sons married women who lived in their town. One son married Orpah. The other son married Ruth.

Naomi, her two sons, Orpah, and Ruth were very happy. But then both of Naomi's sons died. Naomi was very sad. But Naomi knew that God loved her.

Then Naomi heard that the famine was over in the country where she and her family had lived before. She decided to go back to the country she had come from.

So Naomi, Orpah, and Ruth packed their few belongings, sold the animals they had left, and started on their way back to the country Naomi and her family had come from.

After a short time, Naomi said to Orpah and Ruth, "You have been like real daughters to me. But you don't have to come back with me. Go home to your families. May God bless you for being so kind and loving."

Orpah and Ruth began to cry. They loved Naomi very much. Orpah finally decided to do what Naomi suggested. She turned around and went back to the home of her family.

But Ruth said, "Don't ask me to leave you! Where you go, I will go. Where you stay, I will stay. Your people will be my people, and your God will be my God."

Naomi saw how much Ruth loved her. Naomi knew how much God loved her. Together Naomi and Ruth traveled back to the country that Naomi had come from. When they reached Naomi's hometown, Bethlehem, the whole town was excited. "Can this be Naomi?" the people said. Naomi told the people what had happened to her in the country of Moab.

Ruth stayed with Naomi in her land. After a time, Ruth married a man named Boaz. Ruth and Boaz loved each other. They had a baby boy named Obed. Ruth and Boaz loved Naomi. Naomi loved Ruth and Boaz and Obed. And Ruth and Boaz and Naomi loved God.

What shall we pack?

There are many stories in the Bible that tell about God's people going on a journey. The people had to pack many different things when they went somewhere. Play "What shall we pack?" with your child, comparing the kinds of things God's people might have packed for a trip with some of the things people might pack today.

To play, the first person says, "We're going on a trip. What shall we pack?" and then names an item that begins with "A." The next person repeats the "A" item, then adds an item that begins with "B," and so on. Vary this game to suit the ages of your children, perhaps by naming only items that begin with "A."

Prayer to share

Dear God, please keep all people who are in other cities and countries in your loving care. Give them safe journeys when they travel. Amen.

"The Lord was with Samuel as he grew up."   *1 Samuel 3:19*

14 A Boy Named Samuel

1 Samuel 1–4, 7–8

This Bible story is about a boy named Samuel.

There was a woman named Hannah who loved God. More than anything in the world, Hannah and her husband wanted to have a baby.

Because Hannah loved God, she prayed, "O Lord, if you will give me a son, I promise when he is old enough I will give him back to you to work for you in the temple."

God answered Hannah's prayer! When her baby was born, Hannah said, "I will name him Samuel because I asked God for him."

When Samuel was a little boy, Hannah took him to the temple. At the temple, Hannah told the priest Eli about her promise to God. Eli said to Hannah, "I know that you love God. I will keep your son Samuel with me. He can serve God here at the temple."

As Samuel grew, Eli told him about God and God's people. Samuel was happy that he was growing up and learning to love and serve God.

Late one night, when Eli and Samuel were almost asleep, God called out, "Samuel."

Samuel did not know it was God's voice that he heard. Samuel got up from his bed and went to Eli.

"Here I am," Samuel said to Eli. "Did you call me?"

But Eli said, "No, I did not call. Go back to sleep."

After Samuel had gone back to bed, he heard the voice call again, "Samuel."

Quickly, Samuel got up and went to where Eli was sleeping.

"You called me," Samuel said to Eli, "and here I am."

"It was not I calling you," Eli said again. "Go back to sleep."

After Samuel went back to bed, God's voice called him again. This time, when Samuel went into Eli's room, Eli realized that God was calling Samuel.

"Go and lie down," Eli told Samuel. "When you hear God calling, answer, 'Speak, Lord, your servant is listening.' "

Samuel did as Eli told him. When God called again, Samuel answered. And God gave Samuel a message for Eli. Throughout Samuel's life, God gave Samuel messages for all the people and taught him many things. Samuel became a special leader for God's people.

Pretending

Pretend to be Eli and have your child pretend to be Samuel. Act out the story, encouraging your child to use his or her own words. Then switch roles and repeat the story. Ask your child to think about how Samuel might have felt when God called him. Talk about ways God speaks to us today—through the Bible, teachers, pastors, and others.

Prayer to share

Dear God, you are always with us! Thank you for loving us when we are happy or sad, playing or working, awake or asleep. Amen.

43

"Do you see the man the Lord has chosen? There is no one like him among all the people."

1 Samuel 10:24

15   Saul, the King

1 Samuel 9–11, 13–15

This Bible story is about Saul, the king. A young man named Saul lived while Samuel was a leader of God's people. Saul lived with his family in a different part of the country. Saul had heard that Samuel was very wise and that he loved God.

One day, some of the donkeys that belonged to Saul's family wandered away. Saul and his brothers looked everywhere for the lost donkeys.

They looked in the next field—the donkeys were not there. They looked on the hillside—the donkeys were not there. They even looked under the trees by the river—but the donkeys were not there.

Saul's father told Saul, "Take a servant with you. Go everywhere you have not looked before and find the donkeys."

They looked for several days. Then Saul said, "We should go back now! We have been gone for so long, my father will be worrying that we are lost too."

But the servant said, "This is where Samuel lives. Maybe he knows where we can find the donkeys."

Now the day before this, God had told Samuel, "Tomorrow I will send a young man to you. My people want to have a king. You can anoint this man to be the king for my people."

Samuel was looking out his door when he saw Saul and the servant climb the hill. Samuel knew that this was the man God had told him about. Samuel asked the cook, "Please cook a meal for the two men climbing up the hill."

After Saul and the servant had eaten with Samuel, Samuel talked with Saul late into the night. When morning came, Samuel said, "Let your servant leave ahead of you. I will tell him where to find the donkeys. But you stay a little longer so I can tell you a message from God."

Then Samuel told Saul what God had said. Samuel took a bottle of oil and poured it on Saul's head to anoint him.

"You are anointed as king over God's people," Samuel said. "Rule wisely."

"God and me" fingerplay

Explain to your child that God was with Saul every day and night. God is with us every day and night, too. Do this fingerplay together:

God is with me when the sun shines bright. *(Raise arms in a circle over your head.)*
God takes care of me day and night. *(Fold hands and rest your cheek on them.)*
God is with me whenever I play. *(Pretend to throw and catch a ball.)*
God and me together—every day! *(Clap hands.)*

Prayer to share

Dear God, we thank you for your loving care. Give us kind words to share today. Help us to show your love to other people that we know. Amen.

"Therefore I will praise you, O Lord, among the nations; I will sing praises to your name."

2 Samuel 22:50

16 David, the Shepherd Boy and King

1 Samuel 16–17

This Bible story is about David, the shepherd boy and king.

After a time, King Saul did some things that made God unhappy. God spoke to Samuel again and said, "Don't be sad! I am sending you to Jesse, a man in Bethlehem. I have chosen one of his sons to be a king for my people."

Samuel met Jesse and also met seven of Jesse's sons. Samuel asked, "Are these all the sons you have?"

"No," Jesse answered, "the youngest of my sons is with the sheep." When David, the youngest son, came in from the field, Samuel knew this was the son God had told him about. Samuel took a bottle of oil and anointed David to be king someday. And God was with David.

Some time later, King Saul became sick. His servants heard about a shepherd boy.

The shepherd boy loved God.

The shepherd boy was brave.

The shepherd boy could play beautiful music on the harp.

The shepherd boy was David.

The servants asked David to come and play his beautiful music for Saul. When King Saul heard David's music, he felt much better.

One time, David, the shepherd boy, fought a great warrior named Goliath. Goliath was over nine feet tall. He wore a shiny metal helmet on his head. He wore shiny metal all over to protect him.

Although there were many soldiers in King Saul's army, everyone was afraid of Goliath. Goliath was sure that he would win the fight with Saul's army.

But David, the shepherd boy, had protected his father's sheep for many years. He had kept his sheep safe, even safe from wolves at night.

When David heard that no one would fight Goliath, he put five small smooth stones into his pouch. Then he took his slingshot and went to fight Goliath.

Goliath laughed when he saw David. "How can a small shepherd boy like you fight with me?"

David, the shepherd boy, answered, "You bring a sword to fight with, but I bring God's name."

Goliath moved forward to begin the fight. David reached into his pouch and put one of the five small, smooth stones into his slingshot. Then David darted forward. *Ziinngg!* The small stone hit Goliath right in the middle of his forehead and he fell to the ground. Goliath was dead.

After many years, when King Saul died, David became the king for God's people. David was a good king. He loved God and he loved God's people.

"Sing, David, Sing"

Sing the song on page 48 with your child. Talk about David, the shepherd boy who became king.

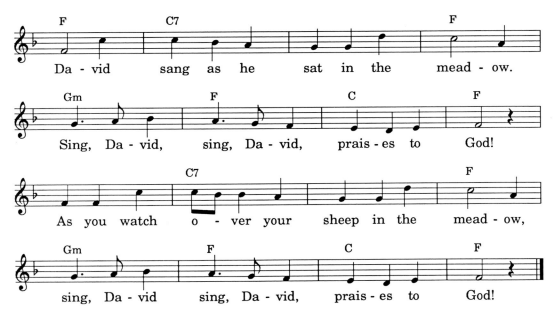

Da - vid sang as he sat in the mead - ow.

Sing, Da - vid, sing, Da - vid, prais - es to God!

As you watch o - ver your sheep in the mead - ow,

sing, Da - vid sing, Da - vid, prais - es to God!

Words: Carol Greene
Music: 14th Century English
Reprinted from *The Little Christian's Songbook* copyright © 1975 Concordia Publishing House. Used by permission.

Prayer to share

Thank you, God, for people like David, people who love you and who love God's people. Amen.

17 The Book of Psalms

Selected psalms, paraphrased

Psalms are poems of praise, worship, and thankfulness to God. King David wrote some of the psalms in the Bible.

O Lord, how great you are!
You are greater than the sun and moon
    and stars in the sky.
Children in all the world praise you.
When I look into the sky, and see the
    moon and the stars you have made,
I am surprised that you care about little
    me.
Yet you put people like me in charge of
    the birds in the air, the animals on land,
    and the fish in the water.
Lord, how great you are!

           (Psalm 8:1-9)

The Lord is my shepherd, I will have what
    I need.
The Lord gives me green grass to lie in
    and quiet waters to drink from.
The Lord leads me in the way I should
    go.
Even if I am frightened, I know the Lord
    is with me.
The Lord loves me and keeps me safe.
The Lord watches over everything that I
    do and blesses me.

Surely the Lord's love will be with me
    always.

           (Psalm 23:1-6)

Sing a new song to the Lord;
sing all the earth!
Sing to the Lord and praise God's name.
Tell everyone the good news of God's love.
Share God's love with people all over the
    world.
Worship and praise the Lord who is holy.
Let the skies and the earth be glad; Let
    the waters sing out. Let the fields be
    jubilant.
Then all the trees in the forest will sing
    for joy to the Lord.

      (Psalm 96, selected verses)

I look up to the hills—where does my help
    come from?
My help comes from the Lord,
    the Maker of heaven and earth.
The Lord who watches over me will keep
    me safe.
The Lord will keep me from harm in any
    part of my life.
The Lord will watch me when I come and
    when I go, today and always.

           (Psalm 121)

Rhythm instruments

Make and use rhythm instruments to accompany your reading of the Psalms. Make a drum from a can that has a plastic lid (a coffee can works well). Cover the can with paper on which your child has drawn designs. Use a wooden spoon for a drumstick. A tambourine can be made from two paper plates and a few pebbles or paper clips. Put a handful of pebbles or paper clips between the two plates and secure with masking tape all around the edges. Draw designs on the plates with felt-tipped

markers and add crepe paper for decoration. Sing together the following song, "Psalm 8." Wherever the asterisk appears in the song, beat your drum or shake your tambourine!

"Psalm 8"

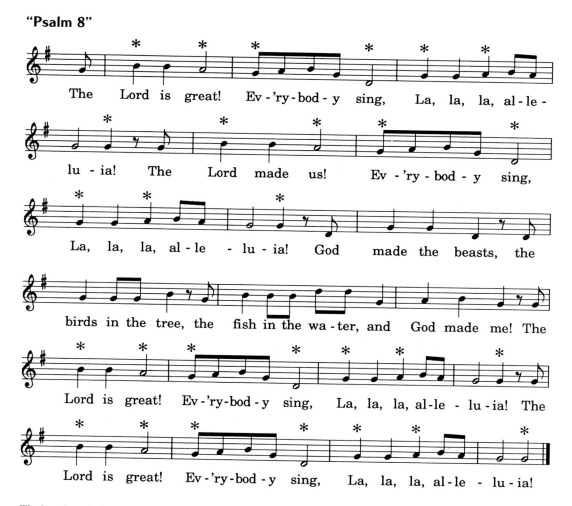

Words and music: John Erickson
Copyright © John Erickson. Used by permission.

Prayer to share

Dear God, we can praise you and sing happy songs to you. You are great and good! Amen.

"A cheerful look brings joy to the heart."   *Proverbs 15:30*

18   The Book of Proverbs

Selected proverbs, paraphrased

The book of Proverbs has wise sayings and good advice written in it. It is believed that King Solomon wrote many of the proverbs.

Here are some of the proverbs you will find in the Bible.

For the Lord gives wisdom, knowledge, and understanding. (Proverbs 2:6)

Trust in the Lord with all your heart and don't trust only your own knowledge. (Proverbs 3:5)

Happy is the person who finds wisdom and understanding; they are better than silver and gold. (Proverbs 3:13-14)

The Lord dislikes lies but is happy when people tell the truth. (Proverbs 12:22)

A gentle answer can stop anger but a harsh word stirs up anger. (Proverbs 15:1)

A cheerful look makes a heart happy and good news helps a person to feel good. (Proverbs 15:30)

A kind word said at the right time is like golden apples in a silver bowl. (Proverbs 25:11)

Do not brag about tomorrow, for you do not know what it will be like. (Proverbs 27:1)

Make a collage

Gather a variety of materials, such as cotton balls, fabric scraps, aluminum foil, corrugated cardboard, and twigs.

Help your child arrange these items in a collage design on a piece of poster board or a paper plate. When you are pleased with the design, glue the items down. Explain that you are making a collage, a collection of many things made into one picture.

As you are working on this activity, talk with your child about the many wise sayings we can read in the Bible. When put together, these wise sayings are like a collage of thoughts that can help us to live a good, happy life.

Prayer to share

Dear Lord, thank you for people who share their wise advice with us. Thank you for choices and the wisdom to choose what is right and good. Amen.

19 Solomon, the Wise King

1 Kings 3, 5—10

This Bible story is about Solomon, a wise king.

King David had a son named Solomon. As he grew, Solomon learned many things from his father David.

David loved God. Solomon loved God.

David served God and loved God's people. Solomon served God and loved God's people.

David worshiped and praised God. Solomon worshiped and praised God.

After King David died, Solomon became the new king. Solomon loved and served and praised God, just as his father had.

One night Solomon had a dream. In Solomon's dream, God said, "Ask me for whatever you want."

In Solomon's dream, he answered God with these words:

"You always loved my father David. Now you have made me king of your people. Please make me wise enough to know what is right and wrong. Then I can serve you and your people."

"I am happy that you have not asked to live a long life or to be rich," God said to Solomon in the dream. "I will make you the wisest person who has ever lived. And because you did not think only of yourself, I will give you riches and honor and long life, too."

When Solomon woke up, he remembered what God had said in his dream. Solomon worshiped and praised God.

From that time on, Solomon was a very wise person. When God's people had a question or a problem they couldn't answer, they came to talk with Solomon. God gave Solomon the wisdom he needed to help people.

A friend of King David's, named Hiram, heard about how wise Solomon was. Solomon told Hiram that he wanted to build a temple. The temple would be for people to worship God. The country where Hiram lived had the kind of trees Solomon needed for the temple. Hiram agreed to sell the trees to Solomon.

When all the wood was cut and piled up, Solomon said, "Let us begin building a temple for the Lord!"

The people worked very hard to build the temple. They cut heavy stones to stack up for the walls. They cut cedar and pine logs for the floors and ceilings. Some of the people carved flowers and leaves in the wood to decorate the temple. Others worked hard to decorate the inside with gold and silver.

After seven years, the temple of the Lord was finally finished. Everyone had worked hard to help Solomon, the wise king, build a temple to praise and worship God.

Building a temple

Collect boxes of assorted sizes and shapes. Help your child to arrange and rearrange the boxes in various ways, working to construct a temple building. As you do this, talk about the time, work, and energy involved in constructing a building. Once you and your child are pleased with the way the temple looks, tape the pieces together with heavy tape. Decorate the boxes using felt-tipped markers or crayons, or cover them with colored paper. Add steps, doors, and windows to complete the temple building.

Prayer to share

Lord, we thank you for the wise people in our lives who show us how to live in your love each day! Amen.

20 Elijah, One of God's Prophets

1 Kings 17:1-16

This Bible story is about Elijah, one of God's prophets.

There were many people who loved and worshiped God. Some were men. Some were women. Some were shepherds and musicians. Others were farmers and cooks. And some of the people were prophets, people who told others how God wanted them to live.

King Ahab, another king of Israel, did not love God in the way other kings before him had. God was not happy with Ahab and the way he ruled over God's people.

Elijah was a prophet who loved God. One day, Elijah came to King Ahab. "God is not happy with you, Ahab," Elijah said.

"What does that matter to me?" Ahab answered.

"In the name of the Lord," said Elijah, "I tell you—there will be no dew and no rain for the next few years unless I say so."

Then God told Elijah, "Leave this place and go east. Hide there by the small river. You will have water to drink and I will have the ravens feed you."

Elijah did what God had told him. He found the small river and hid there. The water in the river was clear and cold and good to drink. And God sent the ravens every morning and every evening with food for Elijah to eat.

After there had been no rain, the river dried up. Then God sent Elijah to a different city.

Elijah's feet made dust clouds as he walked through the hot, dry land. When Elijah reached the city gate, he saw a woman gathering sticks for her fire.

Elijah called to the woman, "Can you bring me some water to drink? I am so thirsty. Please, can you also bring me a piece of bread?"

Then the woman answered Elijah, "Sir, I don't have any bread. I only have a handful of flour and a little oil in a jar. These sticks are for a fire to make a last meal for my son and myself."

Elijah said to the woman, "Don't worry. Go home and make a small loaf of bread for me. Then make something for yourself and your son. God has told me that the jar of flour and the jar of oil will not be used up until the day the Lord makes it rain again."

So the woman went home and did as Elijah said. Just as God promised, there was food every day for Elijah, the woman, and her son.

Caring for God's creatures

Make a simple bird feeder or bird bath to remind you and your child about the ravens God sent to care for Elijah. Remind your child that God cares for all creatures—for people like Elijah and the widow, for us, for animals, for every living thing.

Take a large pinecone, spread it with peanut butter (unsalted is best), and roll it in bird seed. Then hang the pinecone by a string or wire from a tree branch.

A bird bath can be made using a shallow dish such as a saucer from a plastic planter. Knot three 24"-long pieces of heavy string or cord together at each end. Set the saucer into the string, taping the string to the feeder, if necessary. Then fill it with water and hang it from a tree branch.

Be sure to continue leaving bird seed or water (especially in the winter) for the birds once you start. The birds will depend on you.

Prayer to share

For all the creatures that you have made, we thank you, Lord! For birds and animals, fish and bugs, we thank you, Lord! Teach us to care for the creatures in your world in gentle ways, just as you care for us. Amen.

21 Daniel and the Lions

Daniel 6

This Bible story is about Daniel and the lions.

God's people had been taken from their land to a land called Babylonia. The Babylonian people did not worship God. They made it hard for God's people to worship too. But God remembered God's people, even in a strange land.

Darius was king of Babylonia. He was a wise ruler. He chose many people to help him. There were three officials who helped Darius the most. One of these was Daniel. Daniel was one of God's people.

Daniel loved God very much. Daniel was faithful to God even though other people in Babylonia were not.

Every day, Daniel prayed and gave thanks to God.

When Daniel prayed, he got down on his knees.

When Daniel prayed, he folded his hands and bowed his head.

Every day, in the morning, at noon, and in the evening, Daniel prayed and gave thanks to God.

The other officials who helped Darius were jealous of Daniel. They were afraid that Darius would want Daniel to be the ruler over them all. So the other officials tried to find bad things about Daniel to tell Darius. They could find nothing bad. Daniel was a good and honest man. Everyone could trust and respect Daniel.

So the officials planned to trick Darius.

"Oh, King Darius!" the officials said. "We hope you live forever. We have agreed that because you are so important, there should be a new law! The new law will be—people who pray to anyone but you shall be thrown into a den of lions."

Darius agreed with the officials and this became the new law. When Daniel heard this, he went home. There, just as he did every day, Daniel knelt down to pray. With his hands folded and his head bowed, Daniel gave thanks to God.

The other officials had followed Daniel home. When they saw him praying to God, the officials hurried back to tell Darius.

When the king heard what had happened, he was very sad. He thought about how he could save Daniel. But it was no use. When evening came, Daniel was thrown into a den of lions. The king said to Daniel, "May your God, whom you love and serve, save you!"

Later that night, Darius said, "I am not hungry! I am not tired! Nothing can make me feel better. I am worried about my friend, Daniel."

The next morning, when it was just getting light, Darius hurried to the place where Daniel was with the lions. He called out, "Daniel! Daniel—the man who loves God! Has your God saved you?"

The king was overjoyed when he heard Daniel call back to him, "O King, may you live forever! My God sent an angel to shut the lions' mouths. They have not hurt me because God knows I love him. I have been faithful to my God and I have been faithful to you!"

Daniel continued to serve God and King Darius for many years.

Make a lion mask

Use a paper plate as the base for a lion's head mask. Let your child paint or color the plate yellow or gold, if desired. Cut out eyes, a nose, and a mouth and then outline them with crayons or felt-tipped markers. Cut straws from a broom and glue around the nose for whiskers. Cut and curl brown construction paper strips (about 2″ long) for the lion's mane. To curl, roll the paper strips tightly around a pencil, then glue or staple around the edges of the paper plate.

Prayer to share

Dear God, teach us to be faithful and to trust you, as Daniel did. Amen.

22 Jonah and the Big Fish

Jonah 1—4

This Bible story is about Jonah and the big fish.

God had a message for a man named Jonah. "Go to the great city of Nineveh. People in Nineveh have not been living the way I want them to. Warn the people that I will punish them."

Jonah did not want to do what God said. He found a ship that was sailing far away from Nineveh. He paid the captain of the ship so that he could go along. Jonah ran away from God.

Not long after Jonah got onto the ship, a fierce storm came up. The waves rocked the ship more and more. All of the sailors were afraid their ship would sink! Quickly, the sailors threw overboard all the supplies that were on the ship.

The captain of the ship began looking for Jonah. Finally he found him—fast asleep! The captain shook Jonah awake.

"How can you be asleep? Don't you know we might sink?" the captain said. "Wake up and pray to your God. Maybe your God can save us."

The sailors began wondering who Jonah was. "We have never seen this kind of storm before. The waves just keep getting bigger and bigger. Maybe it is your fault."

When Jonah told the captain and the sailors that he was running away from God, they said, "What can we do to make the storm stop?"

"Throw me into the sea," Jonah replied. "Then the waves will stop and you will be safe. This storm is my fault—I didn't do what God told me to do."

The sailors were afraid to throw Jonah into the sea. But they did as Jonah told them. The sea became calm.

Now God made a big fish, as big as a whale, swallow Jonah. Jonah was inside the big fish for three days and three nights. All of the time Jonah was inside the fish, he prayed to God. Jonah prayed, "You always hear me when I pray, Lord. You always save me. I am sorry I ran away from you."

And God made the big fish spit Jonah onto the beach.

God told Jonah again, "Go to Nineveh and tell the people what I have told you."

This time Jonah obeyed God. Jonah walked all through the big city of Nineveh. He told everyone what God had said. And the people of Nineveh believed Jonah. They were sorry that they had not done what God wanted them to do. They began to live good lives, and God decided not to punish them.

But Jonah was angry with God. "Lord," Jonah prayed, "this is why I didn't want to come here! You are a kind, loving God. You did not punish the people of Nineveh, even though they deserved to be punished."

Jonah went outside the city and sat in the hot sun. He hoped God would decide again to punish the people.

God made a plant grow to give Jonah shade. Jonah liked the plant and the shade that it made. But then, a worm killed the plant. Jonah became angrier.

"Why are you angry?" God asked.

63

"My plant that gave me shade has died," Jonah said.

And God told Jonah, "You are sad and angry because a little plant died. Don't you think I would have been more sad if the people of Nineveh and their animals, too, had been lost?"

Jonah thought about what God said. And Jonah knew that God's love was great.

"Jonah"

Sing the following song with your child:

1. God said, "Jo - nah, to Nin - e - veh go!"
2. That poor ship al - most sank in the gale.
3. For three days Jo - nah sat like a stone.
4. Up came Jo - nah, and that's when he thought,

"I'm so sor - ry, God," said Jo - nah, "but no."
Ev - 'ry - thing the sail - ors did seemed to fail
"What a tum - my ache!" he heard the whale groan.
"I'm the first man by a whale to be caught.

Quick he hid in a ship down be - low;
til they tossed Jo - nah o - ver the rail.
"If I spit you back up like a bone,
Strange how God had this les - son be taught;

so God sent a storm and made the wind blow.
Right a - way he was slurped up by a whale.
go to Nin - e - veh, and leave me a - lone!"
but I've learned now, and I'll do what I ought."

Words: Carol Greene   Music: Gluck/Mozart
Reprinted from *The Little Christian's Songbook* copyright © 1975 Concordia Publishing House. Used by permission.

Prayer to share

Dear God, sometimes, like Jonah, we don't feel like loving other people. Help us to love them the way you do. Amen.

"For to us a child is born."   *Isaiah 9:6*

23   Isaiah Tells about God

Isaiah 9:1-7; 11:1-9

This Bible story is about Isaiah and God's messages for the people.

Isaiah, one of God's prophets, told God's people about the plans God had for them.

God wanted people to live in peace. Isaiah knew that God would give people the perfect king to rule them. Isaiah told God's people:

A new king will come from King David's family.

God's spirit will give the new king wisdom and knowledge and skill to rule God's people.

The king will love and obey and praise God. He will judge all people fairly and help those who need it. He will rule God's people wisely.

Then it will be a time of peace, with sheep and wolves living together.

Calves and lion cubs will eat together and little children will take care of them. Cows and bears will live together in peace. Even a baby will be safe if it plays near a poisonous snake.

(Isaiah 11:1-9, paraphrased)

The people in darkness have seen a great light.

People will be joyful and they will live together in peace.

For to us a child is born, to us a son is given, and the government will be on his shoulders.

He will be called Wonderful Counselor, Mighty God, Everlasting Father, Prince of Peace.

His rule and peace will never end.

(Isaiah 9:1-7, paraphrased)

We know now who this wonderful king is that Isaiah spoke about. He is Jesus.

Make peaceful animals

Mix up either of the following two playdough recipes with your child. Then make together some of the animals mentioned in the Isaiah 11 passage. Pretend to have them eat and play together peacefully.

Basic playdough: Sift 3 cups flour, 1½ cups salt, and 6 teaspoons cream of tartar into a saucepan. Combine 3 cups water and 3 tablespoons cooking oil and add them to the dry ingredients, blending well. Add food coloring, a drop at a time, and blend. Cook the playdough mixture over medium heat, stirring constantly until the dough pulls away from the pan. Store the cool playdough in an air-tight container.

Playdough you can eat: Mix ½ cup peanut butter, ¼ cup honey and ½ cup powdered milk in a bowl. Gradually add an additional ½ cup powdered milk until the dough is soft and not sticky.

Prayer to share

Dear God, please teach us to live in peace with people everywhere. Amen.

67

"But the angel said to him . . . 'Your prayer has been heard.' "   *Luke 1:13*

24   The Birth of John

Luke 1:5-25, 57-80

This Bible story is about the birth of John the Baptist.

There was once a priest named Zechariah. Zechariah was married to Elizabeth. Zechariah and Elizabeth loved God very much. Zechariah and Elizabeth loved children. They did not have any children of their own. But they had prayed to God for a child.

When it was Zechariah's turn to go to the temple, he was ready. He was happy to go to burn incense and praise God.

As Zechariah burned the incense, God sent an angel to him.

"Do not be afraid," the angel said. "God has heard the prayer of Elizabeth and you. Now Elizabeth and you will have a son. Name your son John. He will make you happy. He will help people to love God."

"Are you sure?" Zechariah asked the angel.

"God sent me to tell you this," the angel said. "But because you do not be-lieve me, you will not be able to talk until John is born."

When Zechariah went home from the temple, he could not talk. For many months Zechariah could not talk.

When Elizabeth and Zechariah's baby was born, they were happy. Their friends and neighbors were happy. But Zechariah still could not talk.

"Surely you will name your baby Zechariah, after his father," everyone said to Elizabeth and Zechariah.

"No, he will be named John," Elizabeth said.

"But no one in your family has that name!" the people exclaimed.

Then Zechariah wrote a message for everyone to read. The message said: His name is John.

Now Zechariah could talk again! Zechariah and Elizabeth told everyone how happy God had made them. Zechariah sang a song of praise to God. And John grew to love God.

A baby book

Spend time with your child looking at pictures of him or her as a baby. If your child has a baby book, point out pictures or clippings of the place where he or she was born, people who came to visit, and the date of baptism or dedication to God. If you chose your child's name for a particular reason, explain it. Above all, tell your child how happy you were that he or she was born and how you thanked God for such a wonderful gift. Sometime you may want to share your own baby book or early pictures with your child.

Prayer to share

Dear God, thank you for making me special. Amen.

25 Mary, the Mother of Jesus

Luke 1:26-56

This Bible story is about an angel's visit to Mary.

Mary was a woman who loved God.

One day the angel Gabriel came to Mary. This was the same angel who had come to Zechariah.

"Do not be afraid," the angel said. "God is with you. God has something very important for you to do."

Mary wondered what the angel meant by these words.

"God loves you, Mary," the angel said. "And God has blessed you. You will have a son. Name him Jesus. He will be the Son of God."

"I will praise and serve God," Mary said. "I believe what you say."

Then the angel left her.

While she was thinking about what the angel had told her, Mary packed a small bag. She was going to visit her cousin Elizabeth. Mary wanted to tell Elizabeth what the angel had said.

Mary told Elizabeth, "God has blessed me."

Elizabeth was happy for Mary.

Then Mary praised God with words like these:

"I will rejoice because God has blessed me!

"God remembers the people who love him!

"God will always take care of the people who love him!"

And Mary stayed with Elizabeth for three months. Mary and Elizabeth had many things to talk about.

God has blessed me!

Attach a piece of newsprint or poster board to your refrigerator or another central place in your home. Print at the top "God has blessed me!" If you like, divide the paper so that each family member has a section. Work together to print or draw some of the ways God has blessed each of you. Be sure to include the great blessing God gave us in sending Jesus. This can be an ongoing project that will be enjoyed by all family members.

Prayer to share

Dear God, thank you for blessing me with (insert your thoughts here). *Amen.*

26   Jesus Is Born!

Luke 2:1-7

This Bible story is about the night Jesus was born in Bethlehem.

Joseph and Mary had heard the news. Caesar Augustus, the ruler of Rome, had said, "Everyone must go to their hometowns. I want to know how many people there are. Everyone must be counted."

So Joseph and Mary got ready to go to Bethlehem. Joseph put soft blankets across his donkey's back. Mary wrapped food in a bundle. Then she put water into a skin bag. Mary knew that she and Joseph would be hungry and thirsty on the trip to Bethlehem.

Clip-clop, clip-clop.

Step, step, step.

Bump, bump, bump.

Clip-clip, clop-clop went the donkey's hooves.

Step, step, step went Joseph's feet walking beside the donkey.

Bump, bump, bump went Mary on the donkey's back.

Mary was glad that Joseph had put soft blankets on the donkey's back. Mary was going to have a baby. That baby would be God's Son, Jesus.

It was very crowded in Bethlehem. Everyone had heard the news. They had come to be counted.

"Joseph," said Mary. "I am very tired. Can we find a room to stay in?"

"I will ask at this inn," Joseph told Mary. Joseph knew that Mary was tired. He knew that soon Mary would have a baby. That baby would be God's Son, Jesus.

Knock, knock, knock.

Joseph knocked on the door of the inn. When the innkeeper opened the door, he was sad. He did not have an empty room for Joseph and Mary to stay in.

"My inn is full," the innkeeper told Joseph. "But you can stay in my stable. It is warm and dry."

Joseph helped Mary down from the donkey. Then he made a soft bed in the straw for Mary. It was time for Mary's baby to be born.

Mary wrapped her baby in soft, white cloths. Then she laid him in the soft straw in a manger bed.

"Away in a Manger"

Sing "Away in a Manger" with your child, using these motions:

Away in a manger, no crib for his bed, (*Cradle a baby in your arms.*)
the little Lord Jesus laid down his sweet head, (*Fold hands and rest cheek on them.*)
The stars in the sky looked down where he lay, (*Open and close fingers of both hands.*)
the little Lord Jesus asleep on the hay. (*Fold hands and rest cheek on them.*)

Prayer to share

Be near me, Lord Jesus. I ask you to stay, close by me forever and love me I pray. Bless all the dear children in your tender care and fit us for heaven to live with you there. Amen.

"I bring you good news of great joy that will be for all the people."   *Luke 2:10*

27   The Shepherds Visit Jesus

Luke 2:8-20

This Bible story is about the shepherds who came to visit Jesus.

On the night when baby Jesus was born, most people were sleeping. But some shepherds were in the fields near Bethlehem. The shepherds were watching their sheep. It was very quiet. The shepherds watched their sheep and looked up at the twinkling stars in the dark sky.

Suddenly the dark sky got brighter. And brighter. The twinkling stars became a great light. The shepherds were afraid and hid their eyes.

Then the shepherds heard a voice. It was the voice of one of God's angels.

"Don't be afraid," the angel said. "I have good news to tell you. Tonight God's Son, Jesus, was born. He is sleeping in a straw manger bed in Bethlehem."

The shepherds uncovered their eyes. They saw many angels in the sky with the twinkling stars.

The angels sang this joyful song:

"Glory to God in the highest, and peace on earth to people with whom God is pleased."

Just as the sky had gotten brighter, it got darker. And darker. The angels were gone. It was very quiet. The shepherds looked up at the twinkling stars in the dark sky.

"Let's go to Bethlehem," the shepherds said to one another. "Let's go visit Jesus."

The shepherds ran to Bethlehem. They found the stable where the cows and sheep and doves lived. In the stable, Mary and Joseph and the donkey were watching Jesus. Jesus was sleeping in a manger bed of straw. The shepherds watched baby Jesus sleep too.

When the shepherds left the stable to go back to their sheep, they stopped everyone that they saw.

"We have good news to tell you!" the shepherds said. "Tonight God's Son, Jesus, was born in Bethlehem."

An angel to make

Use this simple pattern to make an angel. Enlarge the pattern on firm white paper. Help your child cut the angel out. Bend the angel, forming the base into a circle. Tape the edges together. You and your child may add facial features to the angel if you wish. Make many angels to remind you of the night of Jesus' birth!

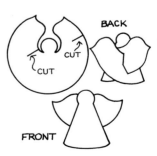

Prayer to share

Dear God, thank you for sending your Son, Jesus. Amen.

28 The Wise Men Who Followed a Star

Matthew 2:1-12

This Bible story is about the wise men who followed a star to find Jesus.

When Jesus was born in Bethlehem, wise men in a far country saw a bright new star in the sky. Each wise man studied the star carefully and thought to himself, "This bright new star means something special. This bright new star means that a new king has been born. I must follow the star to find him. Then I can worship him."

Each wise man thought carefully about what special gift he would take to the new king.

"I will take him gold," said one wise man. "Gold is a gift for a king."

"I will take him incense," said another wise man. "Spicy incense is a gift for a king."

"I will take him myrrh," said another wise man. "Sweet-smelling myrrh is a gift for a king."

After they had chosen their gifts, the wise men climbed up on their camels. They looked for the bright new star in the sky. The wise men followed the star for many days and nights.

When the wise men came to Jerusalem, they asked, "Where is the new king? We saw his bright new star in the sky, and we have come to worship him."

When King Herod heard this, he was surprised and upset. He called in all his wisest teachers and asked them where the new king was to be born.

"In Bethlehem," they replied. "It has been written by the prophets."

King Herod called the wise men to his palace. Then he sent them to Bethlehem to find the new king. "Find him, and report back to me, so I can worship him too," he lied.

The wise men did as King Herod told them to do, and went on to Bethlehem. The star went ahead of them, until it stopped over the place where Mary, Joseph, and Jesus were.

The wise men were so happy they had found Jesus. They knelt down before him and gave him their gifts of gold, incense, and myrrh. They were thankful that God put the bright new star in the sky so they could find Jesus. Then the wise men climbed up on their camels and traveled home. They did not go back to King Herod, because God warned them not to.

"Where cattle and donkeys" fingerplay

Where cattle and donkeys and woolly sheep lay
(Put out hand flat.)
The sweet baby Jesus was born Christmas Day.
(Fold hands and rest cheek on them.)
The shepherds and Wise Men from near and from far
(First hold a staff, then hold your chin as if thinking.)

Had seen the bright light of the wondrous star.
(Point up in the sky.)
With gifts that were precious and worshiping hearts,
(Hold palm up as if to give a gift, then place hands over heart.)
They traveled by foot or by camel or cart.
(Imitate the motions of these.)
They knelt by the baby, their heads bowed in prayer,
(Kneel and fold hands.)
While Mary rocked Jesus with tenderest care.
(Make motions as if rocking a baby in your arms.)

Prayer to share

Dear God, thank you for giving us the most precious gift of all—your Son, Jesus. Amen.

29　Jesus Visits the Temple

Luke 2:41-52

This Bible story is about when Jesus visited the temple in Jerusalem.

Every year Jesus' family went to the city of Jerusalem for a special feast called Passover. God's people celebrated Passover to remind them of the time Moses led God's people out of Egypt.

When Jesus was 12 years old, he went with Mary and Joseph to Jerusalem.

Jesus and his family met many friends and relatives going to Jerusalem. Everyone laughed and talked together. They were happy and excited they were going to Jerusalem.

Finally Jesus and his family reached the edge of the city. Beyond the walls was Jerusalem!

Jesus and his family celebrated the Passover. They ate special foods and listened to the story of Moses leading God's people out of Egypt.

After the Passover celebration, Mary and Joseph and everyone else got ready to go home. After they had walked part way home, Mary looked around.

"Have you seen Jesus?" Mary asked Joseph.

"There are the other children," Joseph said. "He is probably with them."

But that night when they stopped to eat and sleep Jesus was not there! Mary and Joseph asked everyone, "Have you seen Jesus?" No one had. Mary and Joseph were worried. They hurried back to the city to look for Jesus.

Mary and Joseph looked everywhere in the city. They looked in the streets. They looked in the shops. Mary and Joseph asked everyone, "Have you seen Jesus?" But no one had.

Then Mary and Joseph went to the temple. They heard many voices. One of the voices was Jesus'. He was talking to the teachers in the temple.

Mary and Joseph hugged Jesus. "Jesus, we were worried! We looked everywhere for you," they said.

Jesus looked at Mary and Joseph. "Why were you looking for me?" he asked. "Didn't you know I would be here in my Father's house?"

Jesus and Mary and Joseph started the trip home.

Mary and Joseph were glad that Jesus was safe.

Make a scroll

The teachers in the temple had scrolls with God's word written on them. Make a Bible message scroll with your child.

Print a Bible verse or message like "God loves you" on a sheet of white paper. Gently roll the paper up to form a scroll. Tie a piece of ribbon or string around the scroll.

Prayer to share

Dear God, it is good to hear stories about when Jesus was young. Thank you for all the people who help me learn about you! Amen.

30 A Man Named John

Matthew 3:1-17

This Bible story is about a man named John the Baptist.

John was the son of Elizabeth and Zechariah. John's parents had told him stories about God who created the world. They had told him about Noah and Solomon and Ruth. Elizabeth and Zechariah told John about God's prophets and the messages they had for God's people. They knew that God had an important job for John to do.

When John grew up, he went to the hot, dry desert to live by himself. But John knew God was with him. John's clothes were made of camel hair, and he wore a leather belt around his waist. John ate locusts and wild honey in the desert.

John was one of God's prophets. He told people about God's love. He told people that God wanted them to live a good life. God wanted them to help other people. Many people came to see John. They listened to John talk about God. When people heard John's words, they were sorry that they had not lived a good life. They wanted to do better. Then John baptized them in the Jordan River.

"I baptize you with water so you will be forgiven," John said to the people. "But another person is coming who will baptize you in a better way."

One day, Jesus was in the crowd of people who came to hear John talk about God. John knew who Jesus was when he saw him—the special person God had sent.

When Jesus asked John to baptize him, John said, "Why are you here? I should ask you to baptize me!"

But Jesus answered, "Let us do the right thing. You will baptize me."

Because John knew Jesus was sent from God, he agreed.

Jesus came to the middle of the Jordan River where John was standing. As soon as John baptized Jesus, the light became brighter. It was like the sky opened up! A dove flew down from the sky.

Then John and Jesus heard God's voice.

"This is my own Son, whom I love," the voice said. "I am happy with him."

When Jesus and John came out of the river, they knew they would never be the same. John was glad that he had seen God's Son. And Jesus was ready to begin his work.

Water and bubbles

Water is an essential part of all our lives. Set up a sink or dishpan with water for your child to play in. Put an apron or towel on your child so he or she stays dry. Give your child a nonelectric egg beater, funnel, sponges, a baster, or other unbreakable items that are fun to play with in water. Include measuring spoons and cups. After a few minutes with just water, add dishwashing detergent to make suds.

Talk with your child about the ways we use water—to drink, bathe in, wash in, and swim in. Then explain that water is an important part of baptism, a time when we remember how much God loves us. The water reminds us that we are "like new" because God loves and forgives us.

Prayer to share

Dear God, thank you for water—water that cleans us, water that cools us, water that makes us your children. Amen.

31   The Four Fishermen

Luke 5:1-11

This Bible story is about four fishermen who followed Jesus.

After John baptized Jesus, Jesus began to teach people the good news that God loved them. Many people who were sick came to see Jesus because he helped them get better.

Sometimes Jesus became tired from walking and talking. He wanted to go to a quiet place where no one else was. Then he could pray and talk to God. And God could talk to him.

One day Jesus was near a lake. Many people crowded around Jesus to see and hear him.

"Jesus is very special," some of the people whispered. "He makes me happy when he tells me God loves me."

Soon so many people were around Jesus, he climbed into the boat of two fishermen. The fishermen's names were Simon Peter and Andrew.

"Can you row your boat into the lake? Then everyone will be able to hear and see me," Jesus told Simon Peter.

That day, Jesus taught the people more about God's love. Then he said to Simon Peter and Andrew, "Put your net into the deepest water. Let us catch some fish."

"Master," Simon Peter said, "we've been working all night to catch some fish. But I'll try if you say so."

In a short time, Simon Peter and Andrew started to pull the net up. The net was so full of fish they could hardly pull. The net was so full of fish it began to break.

"Come quickly," Simon Peter shouted to another boat of fishermen. "Our net is so full of fish it is going to break!"

The men hurried to help Simon Peter and Andrew.

Pull. Tug. Pull. Tug. The men worked hard to pull the net in. When they had finished, both boats were so full of fish that they almost sank.

When Simon Peter saw his boat full of fish, he was amazed.

Then Jesus said, "Don't be surprised! Come with me. From now on you will be with me and you will catch people."

So Simon Peter and Andrew, and the other fishermen named James and John, rowed their boats to shore. From that day, the four fishermen went with Jesus, teaching God's Word to the people.

"I Will Make You Fishers of Men"

Sing the song on page 87 with your child and do the actions together. As you sing, "I will make you fishers of men . . ." motion as if you are casting a fishing pole and reeling in a fish. When you come to the words "If you follow me . . ." motion as if you want someone to follow. For stanza two, cup your hands around your mouth when you sing "Hear Christ calling" and bring your hand to your heart as you sing "Come unto me." For "I will give you rest," lay your cheek on folded hands, as if sleeping.

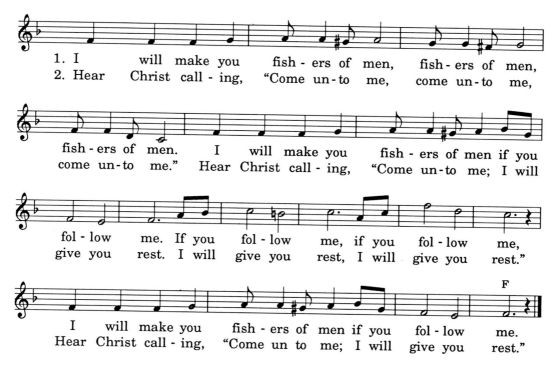

1. I will make you fish-ers of men, fish-ers of men, fish-ers of men. I will make you fish-ers of men if you fol-low me. If you fol-low me, if you fol-low me, I will make you fish-ers of men if you fol-low me.

2. Hear Christ call-ing, "Come un-to me, come un-to me, come un-to me." Hear Christ call-ing, "Come un-to me; I will give you rest. I will give you rest, I will give you rest." Hear Christ call-ing, "Come un to me; I will give you rest."

Words and music: Harry D. Clark

Prayer to share

Dear God, we thank you for people who teach us and people we can teach. Most of all, we thank you for Jesus, the best teacher of all. Amen.

"He (Jesus) called his twelve disciples."   *Matthew 10:1*

32   Twelve Special Friends

Matthew 10:1-42; Luke 6:12-16

This Bible story is about the twelve helpers Jesus chose.

People followed Jesus everywhere. They wanted to hear God's word. But Jesus was only one person. How could he tell everyone about God?

One night, Jesus went to a quiet place. He prayed and asked God what he should do. Jesus prayed all night. Then God answered his prayer.

In the morning, Jesus left the quiet place and went to find his disciples. These disciples would be his special helpers.

When Jesus got to the place where his twelve friends were, he said, "There are still many people who do not know about God's love. You can tell them the good news. You will be my helpers, my disciples."

Jesus' friends were happy! Now they knew how they could help Jesus. They could help Jesus by telling everyone about God's love.

Then Jesus told his twelve friends many things.

"God loves you and forgives you. Trust in God, and do as God asks. You can share God's word with others. Go to the people who have forgotten about God. Tell them what I have told you. Remember, God's love is always with you."

The names of Jesus' twelve helpers were: Simon Peter and his brother Andrew, fishermen James and John, Philip, Bartholomew, Thomas, Matthew the tax collector, another man named James, Thaddeus, Simon the Zealot, and a man named Judas.

Jesus' friends traveled throughout the countryside, telling everyone they met about Jesus and what he had taught them about God.

"Tell all the people" fingerplay

Jesus asked his friends to go everywhere
(Open hands and point outward.)
To tell all the people of God's loving care.
(Act as if you are talking to people, then cross your hands over your heart.)
First Jesus told people, "God loves you! God loves you!"
(Point as if to people then cross hands over heart.)
Then Jesus' friends told people that too.
(Open hands and point outward.)

Prayer to share

Dear God, thank you for promising to love and help us. Like the disciples, we want to share the good news with people we know. Amen.

33 Jesus Teaches the People

Matthew 5:1-12; Luke 6:17-26

This Bible story is about a time when Jesus taught the people.

Many, many people wanted to see Jesus. Many, many people wanted to hear what Jesus had to say. Everywhere Jesus and the disciples went, many, many people followed them.

Sometimes Jesus sat in a boat to teach the people. Sometimes he sat on a hill. Jesus taught people in the cities and in the fields. Wherever people were, Jesus taught them about God's love.

One day, there were so many people with Jesus, he climbed to the top of a hill. Jesus looked down from the hill. Jesus saw sheep in a field. Jesus saw boats in the lake. And Jesus saw all the people looking up at him.

Then Jesus began to teach the people.

"Happy are the poor, for God's kingdom is theirs.

"Happy are the sad, for they will feel better.

"Happy are those who cry, for they will soon laugh.

"Happy are those who make peace, for they will be called God's children."

Everyone listened carefully to Jesus' words. They were happy to hear that God loved them. They were happy they were God's children.

"Rejoice and be glad," Jesus said to all the people, "you belong to God!"

Message line

Hang a short length of string or clothesline somewhere in your house. Clip a number of clothespins to the line. Print some messages about God's love on slips of paper and hang them from the message line. Write messages such as "God loves you" or "You are a special child of God." Your child may want to draw a picture of a favorite Bible story to hang on the line. Use the line for all kinds of messages you want to share with other family members.

Prayer to share

Dear Lord, we are happy to belong to your family! Whenever we laugh, help us remember you. Let us share your love and peace with the people in our families and with our friends each day. Amen.

34   A Boat in a Storm

Mark 4:35-41

This Bible story is about Jesus' friends who were caught in a storm.

Many, many people followed Jesus. They followed Jesus from town to town. Whenever Jesus stopped, the people crowded around him. Everyone wanted to touch Jesus and to hear what he said.

Jesus was tired. He wanted to rest. His friends were tired too. They needed to rest. Jesus saw an empty boat near the lake.

Jesus said to his friends, "Let's get in and row to the other side."

Jesus' friends were glad to get into the boat. It was good to feel the cool breeze as they sat in the boat. It was good to hear the waves lapping against the side of the boat. It was good to feel the waves rocking the boat gently.

Soon Jesus fell asleep. It was quiet in the boat.

Suddenly, everything changed. Black clouds rolled into the sky. Big raindrops splashed into the boat. Thunder crashed. Lightning flashed. The waves splashed and splashed.

Jesus' friends were afraid.

"Jesus! Jesus!" his friends called. "Wake up and help us. We are sinking!"

Jesus woke up. "Don't be afraid. I am with you," Jesus said.

Then Jesus said to the wind, "Stop blowing."

Jesus said to the waves, "Be still."

As soon as Jesus spoke, it was quiet again. The wind stopped blowing. Raindrops stopped falling. Lightning stopped flashing in the sky.

Then Jesus' friends looked at each other. They were surprised. They knew Jesus was God's Son. And now they knew that God gave Jesus the power to stop a storm.

Walnut shell boats

Show your child how to use half walnut shells to make small boats. (If you do not have any walnut shells, you can use jar lids.) Pinch off a small piece of playdough or clay and roll it into a ball. Press the ball into the bottom of the walnut shell. Cut a triangle from a small piece of thin paper and attach it to a toothpick. Insert the toothpick into the playdough ball for a sail. Float the walnut shell boat in a sink or dishpan of water. Show your child how to make wind and waves when he or she is floating the walnut shell boat.

Prayer to share

Dear God, when we are afraid of anything, help us remember how Jesus helped his friends in the storm. Amen.

"They all ate and were satisfied."

35 Five Loaves of Bread and Two Fish

John 6:1–15

This Bible story is about a dinner of five loaves of bread and two fish.

Another time Jesus was teaching many, many people. As he looked out at the crowd, he thought they might be getting hungry.

"These people are getting hungry," Jesus said to his friends. "Where can we buy some bread for them to eat?"

Philip, one of Jesus' friends, said, "It would take a lot of money to feed all of these people! There are more people here than we can count."

But Andrew, another friend of Jesus, said, "I know there is a small boy here who has five small loaves of brown barley bread. He also has two small, silver fish. But that is not enough to feed everyone!"

Jesus said to his friends, "Tell the people to sit down. Then ask the boy to come to me."

Jesus' friends asked the people to sit on the hillside. There were more than 5000 people sitting down!

"Thank you for sharing your brown bread and silver fish with us," Jesus told the boy.

Then Jesus took the brown bread and the silver fish. Jesus thanked God for them, and broke the brown bread and the silver fish into small pieces. Then Jesus' friends gave the pieces of bread and fish to the people to eat.

When everyone was full, Jesus told his friends, "We don't want to waste the brown bread and silver fish that is left over. Take the baskets and gather the extra pieces."

And when Jesus' friends finished, they had 12 baskets full of brown bread and silver fish left over! The people wondered at such a miracle. "Jesus is a very special prophet," they said to one another.

Bread and fish place mats

Give your child a sheet of construction paper and paper scraps to make place mats. Help him or her cut bread and fish shapes from the paper scraps and glue them around the edges of the place mat. Print the words "Thank you, God, for food" in the center of the place mat. To preserve the place mat, cover it with clear adhesive paper. Your child may want to make bread and fish place mats for all of your family members.

Prayer to share

Dear God, thank you for taking care of us. Especially, we thank you for giving us good food to eat. Amen.

"Let the little children come to me."

36 Jesus and the Children

Mark 10:13-16

This Bible story is about Jesus and some children who came to see him.

One day some parents brought their children to Jesus to be blessed. But Jesus' friends thought Jesus was too busy to be bothered with children.

"Don't bring your babies here," they told the mothers and fathers. "Tell your children to leave Jesus alone! He is too busy."

When Jesus heard what his friends said, he was angry. He said to them, "Let the little children come to see me! Don't stop them. God's kingdom belongs to children.

"This is the truth," Jesus said. "Unless you change and love God as children do, you won't be part of God's kingdom."

Jesus picked up the little children, hugged them, and blessed them.

"Jesus Loves Me"

Sing together this familiar song in a new way:

Jesus loves me, this I know,

for the Bible tells me so;

little ones to him belong; they are weak, but he is strong.

Yes, Jesus loves me, (sing 3 times)

the Bible tells me so.

Prayer to share

Dear God, I am so happy that Jesus loves me! Thank you for loving me too. Amen.

37   The Good Neighbor

Luke 10:25-37

This Bible story is about a good deed that one man did for another.

Jesus taught the people many things. Jesus taught the people that God loved them and wanted them to love each other.

Sometimes Jesus taught by telling stories. One day, Jesus told this story about a good neighbor:

A man was traveling from Jerusalem to Jericho. It was a hot day and the road was dry and dusty.

Suddenly, robbers jumped out from behind a big rock. They grabbed the man, took his money and his clothes, and beat him. They left the badly hurt man lying by the dry, dusty road.

The man lay in the hot sun by the dry, dusty road for a long time.

Step. Step. Step.

A priest came walking down the road toward the man. But when the priest saw the man lying in the hot sun by the dry, dusty road, he didn't stop to help. Instead the priest walked by on the other side of the road.

Step. Step. Step.

Another man came down the road. This man was a Levite. A Levite wore special clothes and served God in the temple. But the Levite didn't stop to help the man lying in the sun by the dry, dusty road either.

Then, a Samaritan, a stranger from a different country, came walking down the road. When he saw the man who was hurt, the Samaritan stopped.

The Samaritan gently cleaned the man's wounds with oil and a soft cloth. He put bandages on the wounds and gave the man a drink of cool water. Then the Samaritan helped the man onto his donkey and took him to an inn. At the inn, the man from Samaria paid the innkeeper to take care of the man who was hurt until he was better.

Then Jesus said to the people listening to the story, "Who was the good neighbor?"

"The one who helped the man," the people said.

Jesus told them, "Go and do as he did."

Helping coupons

Talk with your child about the kinds of things you might do together to help someone you know. Walking a dog, raking leaves, washing dishes, baking cookies—all are thoughtful things to do for others. Decide on something you and your child will do for someone else and make a "coupon" to give the person. This is something you may want to do often as a special reminder of God's love for you and for others!

Prayer to share

Thank you, Lord, for the people we know. Show us ways to help them and to share your love and kindness. Amen.

"He (Zacchaeus) came down at once and welcomed him (Jesus) gladly."

Luke 19:6

38   Zacchaeus, a Tax Collector

Luke 19:1-10

This Bible story is about Zacchaeus, a tax collector who was changed by Jesus' love.

As Jesus traveled around telling people about God, he went through many towns and cities. One day he was traveling through the town of Jericho. When people heard that Jesus was coming to Jericho, they lined up on the streets. Everyone wanted to see Jesus!

A tax collector named Zacchaeus lived in Jericho. Zacchaeus was wealthy. He lived in a big house. Many tax collectors had taken more money than they should have from the people. People thought that Zacchaeus did that too. So he didn't have very many friends.

Zacchaeus wanted to see Jesus. But Zacchaeus had a problem. The streets were crowded with people who wanted to see Jesus. And Zacchaeus was too short to see over all the people in the street!

Then Zacchaeus had an idea. He knew where a tall tree was. Zacchaeus ran to the tree and climbed up. He pushed aside the big leaves on the tree so he could see Jesus when he walked by.

When Jesus got to the tall tree, he stopped and looked up. Jesus looked right at Zacchaeus and said, "Zacchaeus, come down from that tree. Today I am going to visit you in your house."

Zacchaeus scrambled to get out of the tall tree. He hadn't thought that Jesus would even talk to him!

Zacchaeus welcomed Jesus into his house. He listened while Jesus told him about God's love. Zacchaeus decided to change the way he was living.

"Lord, here and now I'm going to give half of everything I have to people who are poor. And if I have cheated anybody out of anything, I will pay back four times what I have taken."

Jesus was happy that Zacchaeus decided to change his life.

"Zacchaeus"

Sing together the song "Zacchaeus" on page 102. Act out the story as you sing using these motions:

Zacchaeus was a wee little man . . . *(Hold out hand, palm down close to floor.)*
He climbed up in a sycamore tree *(Alternate hands as if climbing.)*
for the Lord he wanted to see; *(Shade eyes, look down.)*
And as the Savior passed that way, *(Swing arms as if walking.)*
he looked up in the tree. *(Shade eyes, look up.)*
And he said, "Zacchaeus, you come down." *(Beckon with hand.)*
"For I'm going to your house today." *(Clap in rhythm.)*

101

Zac - chae - us was a wee lit-tle man, a wee lit-tle man was he, he climbed up in a syc - a - more tree for the Lord he want-ed to see; and as the Sav-ior passed that way, he looked up in the tree, and he said: "Zacchaeus, you come down, for I'm go - ing to your house to - day, for I'm go - ing to your house to - day."

Prayer to share

Dear God, help me live the life that you want me to. Amen.

39   The Lost Sheep

Luke 15:1-7

This Bible story is about a shepherd and a lost sheep.

Jesus and his disciples went throughout the countryside telling the people about God. Sometimes Jesus healed sick people. Other times he preached to the people. Sometimes Jesus told the people stories. The stories were called parables.

One day, as Jesus taught the people, some of them began to grumble, "Jesus welcomes people who are sinners. He even eats with them!"

When Jesus heard what they said, he told them this story:

What if you were a shepherd who had 100 sheep, and when you were counting your sheep—one, two, three—you only counted to ninety-nine. Ninety-nine? One sheep was missing!

So you counted the sheep again. But you still had only 99 sheep. Then you would leave your 99 sheep and go to look for the one that was lost.

First you would look in the grassy fields. Then behind the gray rocks. Where was your one lost sheep? You would look behind the trees and by the river. You would look everywhere for your one lost sheep.

Then, listen! *Baa, baa.* The one lost sheep! When you found the one sheep that was lost, you would be so happy! You would lift your sheep onto your shoulders and run home to tell your friends and neighbors.

You would celebrate, and you would say, "Rejoice and be happy with me—I have found my sheep that was lost."

Then Jesus told the people who were listening, "It is the same with God. When someone who has forgotten God, who is lost, changes how he or she is living and returns to God, God is so happy that there is a celebration in heaven!"

"A Little Woolly Lamb"

Sing the song "A Little Woolly Lamb" on page 105 with your child. Then play a hide-and-seek game, taking turns being the lamb and the shepherd. You may wish to play the game as you sing. The "lamb" hides as you sing stanza one; the "shepherd" seeks during stanza two; and the two hug each other as stanza three is sung.

Remind your child of how happy God is when one who is lost has been found, just as the shepherd was happy to find his sheep.

Prayer to share

Dear God, you love us just as the shepherd loves the sheep. Thank you! Amen.

1. A   lit - tle wool - ly lamb went   run - ning off pell -
2. The   shep herd looked a - round, said "Wool - ly lamb is
3. He   found the wool ly lamb by   fol - low - ing his

mell. Then he got   lost and   night - time fell.
lost. I'll find my   lamb at   an - y   cost."
track. The   oth - er sheep said, "Wel - come back!"

Words: Carol Greene
Music: Gluck/Mozart
Reprinted from *The Little Christian's Songbook* copyright © 1975 Concordia Publishing House. Used by permission.

40   The Lost Coin

Luke 15:8-10

This Bible story is about a woman and a lost coin.

One day Jesus told this story:

There was a woman who had 10 silver coins. One, two, three, four, five, six, seven, eight, nine, ten.

One day the woman noticed she had only nine. One, two, three, four, five, six, seven, eight, nine. One coin was lost!

The woman lit a lamp. She looked in every corner of the room. The lost coin was not there.

She looked under the table. The lost coin was not there.

She looked under the bed. The lost coin was not there.

Then the woman got her broom. Carefully the woman swept the floor. Her eyes looked everywhere for the lost coin.

At last she found the coin! The woman was happy. She counted all her silver coins again. One, two, three, four, five, six, seven, eight, nine, ten.

"Come quickly, come quickly," the woman called to her friends and her neighbors. "Rejoice and be happy with me! I have found the coin that was lost." And her friends and her neighbors and everyone who knew the woman was happy with her.

Then Jesus told the people who were listening, "It is the same with God. When someone who has forgotten God, who is lost, returns to God, God is so happy that there is a celebration in heaven!"

Coin clue game

Hide 10 coins around a room. Then write simple clues on notecards to help your child find the coins, as in a treasure hunt. Depending on your child's age, you may also want to include pictures with your clues to make it easier. Once your child has found all the coins, do something special with them, such as save them to put in the offering at church.

As a variation of this game, hide only one coin. Then hide a series of "clue" cards, each one leading the child to the next, and ultimately to the coin. For example, a card might read "Take three steps from the table," at which point the child finds another card with another clue. Talk about the story as you play the game.

Prayer to share

Dear God, help us to be loving and kind to people, especially people who may have forgotten about your love. Amen.

41   The Lost Son

Luke 15:11-32

This Bible story is about a lost son and a loving father.

Another time, Jesus told this story:

There was a man who had two sons. One day, the youngest son said, "Father, give me my share of money." And his father did.

Soon the youngest son left home and went to live far away in another country. While he was there, the son spent all of his money. He had to get a job. The only job he could get was feeding pigs.

But the son still did not have much money. Sometimes he was so hungry he wanted to eat what the pigs were eating.

Then he said to himself, "My father never lets people go hungry! I can go home and tell him I am sorry. Maybe he will let me work for him. At least then I will have enough to eat."

So the youngest son started to travel home.

When the father saw his son coming down the road, he was so happy. He didn't think he would ever see his youngest son again, so he ran to him and hugged him.

Just as he had said, the youngest son told his father he was sorry for what he had done.

Then the father fed the youngest son good food. The father gave the youngest son new clothes. And the father had a party for the youngest son to celebrate that he had come home.

"Listen," the father told everyone, "My son was lost but now he is found!"

The people who were listening to Jesus' parable remembered what Jesus had told them. In the stories about the lost sheep and the lost coin, Jesus had said, "God is so happy when someone who has forgotten him returns to God!" And the people knew it was the same with this story that Jesus told them.

A celebration

Plan a family party or celebration for no other reason than that you love and care for each other. Include refreshments that your children can help prepare, decorations such as balloons, streamers, and flowers, and a special message or card for each person. Play joyful music or sing songs at your celebration!

Prayer to share

Dear God, we thank you for families who love and take care of us. And we thank you that you love us so much. Amen.

"For where your treasure is, there your heart will be also." *Matthew 6:21*

42 A Woman Who Loved God

Luke 21:1-4

This Bible story is about a woman who showed with a simple gift that she loved God.

Jesus was sitting in the temple teaching people. Jesus and his friends told people how much God loved them. They told people about the kind of life God wanted them to live.

One day, as Jesus was teaching, he looked up and saw a line of people climbing the temple steps. There were many different people. Jesus could see that most of the people were very rich. But at the end of the line was a poor woman.

As the rich people came into the temple, they left gifts of money for God. When the woman came into the temple, she left two small copper coins for God. Then she quietly walked away.

When Jesus saw what the woman did, he was happy. He knew that this woman loved God very much.

"This is the truth," Jesus said to his friends. "This poor woman has given more to God than all of the rich people. They gave large gifts to God because they are rich. But she is poor. She gave God all the money she had."

Jesus' friends, the disciples, thought about what Jesus said. And they knew that the woman loved God very much.

Coin can

Save a can with a plastic lid on it. Cut a slit in the lid that is large enough for a quarter to fit through. Have your child decorate a piece of paper with crayons or felt-tipped markers to fit around the can. When he or she finishes, fasten the paper to the can, then cover it with clear adhesive paper to make it more permanent.

As you are working together on this activity, discuss how you might save money for a special offering, perhaps to donate to a local food bank or community organization that helps the needy. Place the completed can somewhere where your family can see it often and be reminded to share God's love by helping other people.

Prayer to share

Dear Lord, thank you for being a gentle teacher. Remind us that our little gifts can show love. Amen.

43 A Special Prayer

Luke 11:1-13

This Bible story is about a prayer that Jesus taught his disciples.

"Look, here comes Jesus," one of Jesus' friends said. "He has been praying. I want to know how to pray as Jesus does."

When Jesus was with his friends, they asked him, "Please teach us how to pray. We want to know how to talk to God like you do."

"These are the words of a special prayer," Jesus answered.

"Father in heaven,
may everyone honor your name.
May your kingdom come.
Give us each day
all that we need.
Forgive us when we
do something wrong
and help us to
forgive everyone else
who does something wrong.
And keep us safe from evil. Amen."

Then Jesus told his friends a story about prayer.

"What if you had a friend who came knocking at your door late at night. Your friend wanted to borrow some bread from you. But you and your family were in bed. Even though you don't want to get up and give your friend the bread, if he keeps knocking, you will get up and give it to him."

"It is like this story when you pray to God," Jesus told his friends. "If you ask, God will give you what you need. If you look, you will find what you are looking for. Because God loves you, you can pray for what you need. And God will give you everything that you need."

Jesus' friends were happy that Jesus had taught them how to pray to God.

A picture prayer

Have your child cut from magazines pictures of objects or other things that might fit into a picture prayer. Look for things like food, clothing, and other items used every day, as well as people or nature scenes. As you are cutting out the pictures, talk about how God provides everything that we need to live.

To make a picture prayer, choose some of your favorite pictures. Think about what kind of prayer you could write, inserting these pictures for words. For example: Thank you, God, for *(food picture)* that helps our bodies stay healthy. Please help *(people picture)* who are hungry. Amen.

Prayer to share

Use your picture prayer for a special family prayer at a meal or at bedtime.

"I am the good shepherd."   *John 10:11*

44   The Good Shepherd

John 10:1-18

This Bible story is about Jesus, the Good Shepherd.

In Jesus' time there were many flocks of sheep. The flocks of sheep all had shepherds. A shepherd took care of the sheep and kept them safe. Many stories in the Bible are about sheep and shepherds.

One day, Jesus explained how he was like a shepherd.

"The shepherd comes into the sheep pen through the gate. When the shepherd calls the sheep, they come running. All of the sheep know the shepherd's voice and they are happy the shepherd is there."

Jesus said, "Then the shepherd takes the sheep out of the pen. The shepherd finds good green grass for the sheep to eat. The shepherd finds cold clean water for the sheep to drink. The sheep follow the shepherd because they know the shepherd's voice."

Then Jesus told the people who were listening to him, "I am the shepherd. You are my sheep. A good shepherd loves and cares for the sheep. A good shepherd is willing to risk his life for the sheep. I love and care for you. The good shepherd makes sure the sheep have good green grass to eat. The good shepherd makes sure the sheep have cold clean water to drink. I make sure that you have everything that you need."

"I am the good shepherd," Jesus said again. "My sheep will know me and they will follow me. I will give my life for my sheep."

Some of the people understood what Jesus was talking about. But some of the people did not.

A soft lamb

Enlarge this simple drawing of a lamb shape or have your child draw his or her own lamb shape on a sheet of white construction paper. Have your child draw the lamb's face and feet on the paper, then fill in the body by gluing white cotton balls inside the lamb's body. If you like, attach a magnetic strip to the back of the lamb so you can hang it on your refrigerator.

Prayer to share

Dear God, we love you! Thank you for sending Jesus, the Good Shepherd, to us. Help us to always know his voice. Amen.

115

"Blessed is he who comes in the name of the Lord!" *Matthew 21:9*

45   A Parade to Welcome Jesus

Matthew 21:1-11

This Bible story is about a parade the people had to welcome Jesus to Jerusalem.

Jesus and his friends were on their way to Jerusalem. Jesus said to two of his friends, "Go to the next town. Look for a donkey and her colt. Untie them and bring them back to me. If the owner asks what you are doing, tell him I need the donkey and her colt."

Jesus' friends went to the next town. They found the donkey and her colt that Jesus had told them about. Jesus' friends untied the donkey and her colt and brought them back to Jesus.

Then Jesus' friends took off their coats and put them on the donkey's back. The coats made a soft seat for Jesus to sit on.

When Jesus came down the raod to Jerusalem, many people were there waiting for him. The people were happy. They welcomed Jesus. Some people cut branches from the palm trees and laid them on the road in front of Jesus. Other people took off their coats and laid them down to make a path for Jesus and the donkey.

Some people waved palm branches and shouted, "Hosanna! Hosanna!"

A few people ran ahead on the road to tell everyone, "Jesus is coming! Jesus is coming!"

Everyone joined the hosanna parade to welcome Jesus to Jerusalem. They shouted, "Blessed is he who comes in the name of the Lord! Hosanna!"

A hosanna parade

Plan your own hosanna parade. Cut "palms" from green construction paper or use green leaves from your yard.

To make palms, cut a leaf shape as shown, then fringe the edges.

Involve other family members if you wish, saying these words as you parade together: "Hosanna, hosanna, our happy voices sing. Hosanna, hosanna, for Jesus is our King!"

When you are done with your parade, place your palms over the main doorway to your home as a reminder that Jesus comes every day as an unseen guest. Whenever you see the palms, rejoice and welcome Jesus!

Prayer to share

Dear God, thank you for sending Jesus who is always with us. We celebrate your name and your love. Thank you, too, for happy times when we can laugh and sing! Amen.

"Do this in remembrance of me."   *Luke 22:19*

46   A Night When Jesus Was a Servant

Luke 22:7-23; John 13:1-17

This Bible story is about a night when Jesus did a servant's job.

It was the night of the Passover, when God's people remembered how God helped them escape from Egypt. Everything was ready for Jesus and his disciples to celebrate the feast.

In an upstairs room in a house, a table was set. There were 13 dishes, one for Jesus and one for each of his friends. Roast lamb, flat bread, and wine were on the table too.

Jesus and his friends gathered around the table. Jesus thanked God for this time together with his friends.

Suddenly, Jesus got up from the table. He wrapped a towel around his waist. He poured clean water into a bowl. Then, Jesus knelt down in front of Peter.

"Lord," Simon Peter asked, "are you going to wash my feet? I should wash your feet! It is a servant's job to wash the master's feet!"

"You do not know now why I am washing your feet, but someday you will. If you want to follow me, you will let me wash your feet," Jesus said.

Jesus washed all of his friends' feet. He wiped them gently with a towel tied around his waist.

When Jesus finished, he said to his friends, "I have been your teacher and friend. But I am also your helper. You must be helpers to each other too."

Jesus sat down at the table again. He picked up a cup of wine and thanked God for it. "Share this wine," Jesus said.

Then Jesus took the flat bread. Jesus thanked God for the bread and he broke it. Jesus gave each of his friends a piece of bread. "Share this bread," Jesus said, "and remember me."

After that, every time Jesus' friends shared bread and wine, they remembered Jesus as he had told them to. They remembered especially what Jesus was going to do for them very soon.

Jesus reminder wheel

Talk with your child about the ways we remember Jesus, answering questions your child may have about the communion practice you are familiar with. Make a reminder wheel showing some of the ways you remember Jesus.

You will need two paper plates of equal size. Cut a pie-shaped wedge in one plate as shown. Divide the other paper plate into pie-shaped wedges the same size as the cut wedge. Help your child draw in the wedges some of the ways we can remember Jesus. Fasten the plates together with a brass fastener. Then turn the wheel together and talk about the different ways we remember Jesus.

Prayer to share

Dear Jesus, thank you for the many ways we can know and remember you. Amen.

"For God so loved the world that he gave his one and only son, that whoever believes in him shall not perish but have eternal life."   *John 3:16*

47 Jesus' Trial and Death

Mark 15:1-47; Luke 22:47—23:56

This Bible story is about the day that Jesus died.

It was very early in the morning, so early that it was still dark. One of Jesus' friends had told some soldiers where Jesus was. The soldiers went to a garden where Jesus and his friends were praying. They arrested Jesus and took him away to the priest's house.

The priests met together. They wanted to get rid of Jesus. The priests were angry that Jesus said he was God's Son. They thought Jesus should die, but they had no power to sentence him. So they sent Jesus to Pilate, the governor.

Pilate asked Jesus many questions. Then Pilate said, "This man, Jesus, hasn't done anything wrong. I think he should go free."

But the priests did not want Jesus to go free. They wanted Pilate to crucify Jesus. Finally Pilate agreed.

The soldiers made fun of Jesus. They put a purple king's robe on him. The soldiers made Jesus wear a crown of sharp, prickly thorns.

Then the soldiers made another man carry a heavy wooden cross to a hill. The cross was what Jesus would be crucified on.

When Jesus was nailed to the cross, the soldiers laughed at him again. A robber hanging on a cross next to Jesus laughed too.

But another robber on the other side of Jesus said, "Jesus, remember me when you are in your kingdom." Jesus promised that the man would be with him in heaven.

Jesus died. Many people were sad. They didn't understand that Jesus died so all our sins would be forgiven.

A man who had a burial cave took Jesus' body down from the cross. This man wrapped Jesus' body in cloths and laid him in the cave. A big stone was rolled in front of the doorway. Jesus' body was buried in the cave.

Cross necklace

Talk with your child about the symbol of the cross. Explain that when Jesus died on the cross and rose again, God's promise of salvation was fulfilled. Read John 3:16. Whenever we see a cross we are reminded of God's great love for us and God's forgiveness.

Help your child make a cross necklace to wear. Cut a cross from construction paper or poster board. Let your child decorate the cross with crayons or felt-tipped markers. Punch a hole at the top of the cross and string a length of yarn through it to form a necklace.

Prayer to share

Dear God, thank you for loving us so much that you sent your Son Jesus to die for us. Amen.

48   Jesus Is Alive!

Mark 16:1-8; Luke 24:1-12

This Bible story is about the first Easter, when Jesus rose from the tomb.

Jesus' friends were very sad. They loved and trusted God. They knew Jesus loved and trusted God. But Jesus' friends didn't understand why Jesus had to die. They missed talking to Jesus. They missed hearing the things Jesus told them about God's love.

On the second morning after Jesus died, some of his friends got up very early. They wanted to do something special to remember Jesus. The women mixed up sweet smelling spices and perfume. Then they started walking to the cave where Jesus' body was.

Step. Step. Step. It was very quiet walking on the road this early in the morning.

Chirup. Chirup. The birds were just starting to wake up.

The women finally reached the place where Jesus' body was buried.

"Look," one woman whispered, "the stone is rolled away!"

The women ran to look inside the cave. Jesus' body was not there!

The women were afraid. They saw a young man dressed in dazzling white clothes sitting on a rock.

"Don't be afraid," the young man said. "I know you are looking for Jesus. He is not here — he is risen! Jesus is alive! Go quickly and tell all of his friends the good news."

The women ran as fast as they could to tell Jesus' friends. Jesus was alive! It was the first Easter.

"Jesus lives" fingerplay

Tell the news, tell the news! *(Lean to the left, hands cupped at mouth.)*
Jesus lives! Jesus lives! *(Open arms wide.)*
Share the joy, share the joy! *(Lean to the right, hands cupped at mouth.)*
Jesus lives! Jesus lives! *(Open arms wide)*
We were sad, *(Make a sad face.)*
but now we're glad—*(Make a happy face.)*
because Jesus lives! *(Open arms wide)*

Prayer to share

Dear God, we are so glad each time we remember that Jesus lives! Thank you for loving us so much that you gave Jesus to us. Amen.

49   A Rushing Wind

Acts 2:1-41

This Bible story is about the Holy Spirit.

After Jesus rose from the dead, he returned to his Father in heaven. Jesus' friends missed him very much. Sometimes they talked to each other about the things Jesus had said. They remembered the stories Jesus told them. Other times they prayed together.

One day, Jesus' friends were all together in one room. Suddenly, there was a sound like a rushing wind in the room. Jesus' friends were afraid. Then they saw what looked like flames of fire resting on them. And they were filled with the Holy Spirit, God's special power. They began to speak in languages they did not know.

Peter went outside with the rest of Jesus' friends. Many people from many nations were in the streets of the city. The people were surprised to hear Jesus' friends speaking in their own languages. "What does this mean?" they asked one another.

Peter stood up on the steps and told everyone: "Listen to this: Jesus is God's Son! God sent Jesus to help you know God better. Even though Jesus died, now he is alive!"

The people who were in the crowd asked Peter, "Now what shall we do?"

"Change your lives and be baptized," Peter answered. "Jesus died so your sins would be forgiven. When you are baptized, you will receive God's special power—the Holy Spirit."

And on that day, called Pentecost, more than 3000 people believed in Jesus and were baptized.

Wind chimes

Make wind chimes as a reminder of the first Pentecost. Save the lids from cans of frozen juice concentrate. (These are the cans with a pull strip.) Wash the lids. Place each on a piece of wood and pound a nail through the top and the bottom with a hammer.

When you have punched six or more lids, let your child decorate them with paints or stickers. Then tie them together with yarn or string. Attach all of the lids to a dowel or stick. Hang the wind chime where the wind will blow it, reminding you of the power of the Spirit who makes things happen, as the wind does.

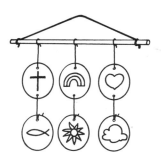

Prayer to share

Thank you, God, for the gift of the Holy Spirit. Let your gift always give me power to believe, to love, and to witness to your love for me. Amen.

50　The Church Long Ago

Acts 2:42-47

This Bible story is about the church long ago.

Jesus' friends told everyone about him. Jesus' friends wanted people everywhere to know that God loved them. They wanted people everywhere to have joy and live the life God wanted them to.

In the church long ago, Jesus' friends taught the people what Jesus had taught them.

The people in the church prayed together.

The people in the church loved each other.

The people in the church helped each other.

If someone was hungry, the people in the church shared their food.

If someone needed clothes or a place to live, the people in the church helped them. The people in the church learned to be helpers, just as Jesus had told his friends to do.

Whenever the people in the church drank wine or ate bread together, they remembered Jesus as he had told them to.

Every day more and more people saw how happy God's people were. More and more people changed their lives to live as God's people too. And God loved them very much.

"Here is the church" fingerplay

Here is the church.
(Fold hands with fingers inside.)
Here is the steeple.
(Point index fingers up together.)
Open the doors.
(Push thumbs apart.)
And see all the people.
(Wiggle the inside fingers.)
Close the doors,
(Put thumbs together.)
And hear them pray
(Put hands to ears.)
Open the doors,
(Put thumbs apart.)
And they all walk away.
(Fingers all walk away.)

Prayer to share

Dear God, thank you for giving us the church—people to share your love with. Amen.